Humility Matters

Humility Matters

for Practicing the Spiritual Life

MARY MARGARET FUNK, O.S.B.

continuum

NEW YORK • LONDON

2007

The Continuum International Publishing Group Inc
80 Maiden Lane, New York, NY 10038

The Continuum International Publishing Group Ltd
The Tower Building, 11 York Road, London SE1 7NX

www.continuumbooks.com

Library of Congress Cataloging-in-Publication Data

Funk, Mary Margaret.
    Humility matters for practicing the spiritual life / Mary Margaret
Funk.
        p.   cm.
    Includes bibliographical references.
    ISBN-13: 978-0-8264-1728-2 (hardcover : alk. paper)
    ISBN-10: 0-8264-1728-0 (hardcover : alk. paper)
    1. Humility—Religious aspects—Catholic Church.   2. Spiritual life
—Catholic Church.   I. Title.
BV4647.H8F86 2005
241'.4—dc22
2005028899

Contents

Foreword

Sister Margaret Funk has been a friend for many years, and I have a great admiration for the enthusiastic spirit she has brought to her work to demonstrate the relevance of the contemplative life in our contemporary world. In this third book in a series devoted to recovering ancient techniques for contemplatives today, she has focused on humility.

All the major world religions are concerned with helping individuals to become good human beings. All emphasize love and compassion, patience, tolerance, forgiveness, humility, and so forth, and all are capable of helping individuals to develop them. I believe that the great spiritual teachers of the past, in addition to conducting themselves with great simplicity, voluntarily accepted suffering—without consideration of the hardships involved—in order to benefit humanity as a whole. They placed special emphasis on developing love and compassion and renouncing selfish desires. And each of them called on us to transform our hearts and minds. This is one of the ways we can make our lives meaningful.

One of the goals of contemplative practice is to lessen the power of negative emotions. If we wish to do this we must search for the causes that give rise to them. We must work at removing or uprooting those causes. At the same time, we must enhance the mental forces that counter them: what we might call their antidotes. This is how a contemplative must gradually bring about the mental transformation he or she seeks. The opposing factor of humility is pride or vanity, while the opposing factor of generosity is stinginess. After identifying such factors, we must endeavour to weaken and undermine them.

Humility is an essential ingredient in our pursuit of transformation although this may seem to be at odds with our need for confidence. But just as there is clearly a distinction between valid confidence, in the sense of self-esteem, and conceit, so it is important to distinguish between genuine humility, which is a kind of modesty, and a lack of confidence. They are not the same thing at all, though many confuse them. This may partly explain why today humility is often thought of as a weakness rather than as an indication of inner strength. Certainly, modern society does not accord humility the place it had in Tibet when I was young. Yet in contemporary life, humility is more important than ever. Just as compassion is of little value if it remains merely an idea, it must become our attitude toward others, reflected in all our thoughts and actions, so the mere concept of humility does not diminish our arrogance; it must become our actual state of being.

This is why Sister Meg is quite correct in saying that humility matters. It is a reflection of our putting others first and placing less importance on ourselves. I trust that readers will find much inspiration in this book and pray that those who do will meet with success in putting that inspiration into effect. Indeed, they might also find encouragement in the following verses from a Tibetan text called *The Eight Verses for Training the Mind* that I think may be relevant here and that I myself have recited since I was a small boy:

> Whenever I am in the company of others,
> May I regard myself as inferior to all
> And from the depths of my heart,
> Cherish others as supreme.

> In all my actions may I watch my mind
> And as soon as disturbing emotions arise,
> May I forcefully stop them at once,
> Since they will hurt both me and others.

The Dalai Lama

August 15, 2005

Introduction

H umility matters. Since God is our heart's desire, we long
for our own direct experience of God. Our world is suffering. Indeed, the root of most of the anguish on earth is the human ego in
denial of its true vocation: to renounce our false self and to embrace
our baptismal initiation into Christ Jesus.

How we labor to empty ourselves of all that is not God in imitation of Jesus is a central concern of the Christian life and has been
the subject of the teaching of spiritual masters since the beginning
of "The Way." In particular, the early ascetics of the Christian tradition were committed to radical discipline in the service of psychic
transformation, because they knew well the truth that is surprisingly
found through the low door of humility.

This book is the third in a series intended to recover traditional
early monastic teachings for contemporary contemplatives. *Thoughts
Matter* retrieved the foundational teaching on the eight afflictive
thoughts that drive the "old nature" in its ambling forgetfulness:
food, sex, things, anger, dejection, acedia, vainglory, and pride. *Tools
Matter* set out the practices that were antidotes to those afflictions.
This volume, *Humility Matters,* takes the spiritual journey full circle
and offers a simple and systematic rendering of monastic teaching
on purity of heart and its human face: humility.

Humility matters. It is at the core of our experience of life in
Christ. So central is this quality of being that it may be said that
humility is for a Christian what enlightenment is for a Buddhist,
realization is for a Hindu, sincerity is for a Confucian, righteousness
is for a Jew, surrender is for a Muslim, and annihilation is for a Sufi.
Humility is what others see of our purity of heart.

Today the world is blessed with contemplatives, some living in monastic communities and perhaps more living anonymously hidden in the world. I offer this book to all spiritual seekers who desire the liberating transformation revealed to us by our elders. Their teachings are classic, timeless, and universal, transcending specific faith traditions. The elders were inspired masters whose inspirations come down to us through a transmission across the generations. We enter into the depths of this wisdom through the prayerful metabolism (rumination) of the gospels, the sayings, conferences, rules, and commentaries. The most important step is not reading but living it, even when it is not before our eyes.

Because there is a systematic progression in the life-changing wisdom spelled out in this modest volume of ancient insight, it is best to read the entire book, then give ourselves years to live into these teachings gradually over the course of our life. In fact, this is what we do with our precious life—follow the movement of what the early Christian teachers called the four renunciations. What becomes evident, as one opens to this wisdom, is that Christian life is always and ever a labor of *conversatio morum*—the ongoing conversion of mind, heart, and way of life that is the real work of the gospel way. This book makes the claim that humility is the unmistakable character of one who has accepted the vocation to take the spiritual journey. So let us begin.

> Come to me, all you that are weary and are carrying heavy burdens, and I will give you rest. Take my yoke upon you, and learn from me, for I am gentle and humble of heart, and you will find rest for your souls. For my yoke is easy and my burden is light. (Matt 11:28–30)

The ancient monastic tradition tells us to undergo four renunciations. First, we renounce our former way of life; second, we renounce the thoughts and desires of our former way of life. Then a deeply felt grace invites us to renounce our self-made thoughts of God. Finally, before the God who is Mystery, we see the light and are enabled to renounce our self-made thoughts of self. Each of these renunciations leads us further into a purity of heart that is experienced in this body, in this lifetime, and is an actual experience of peace. Purity of heart manifests as humility, which is the fruit of the virtuous life.

It makes sense to learn an intelligent way to navigate the spiritual journey from our elders. As rendered here, the spiritual journey proceeds in stages, beginning with the four-fold renunciations, leading to the way of humility. However, an individual would not necessarily travel in a straight sequence in any programmed sense, since God's way is a mystery for each soul. There is more often than not an experience of the simultaneity of all four renunciations. It seems that each of us is invited to taste and see the ancient wisdom for ourselves. This is the reversal of the arrogant tasting and eating in the Garden of Eden, which was a bold striking out to do it alone. In following the way of renunciation, we embrace the wisdom of the ancients. So, let's continue with the catechesis on the four renunciations.

"Negate nothing," say the early masters of the Christian way. Though it may seem ironic, it is important to understand this in the practice of renunciation. Nothing is negated. What is, is! We acknowledge the reality of all that we are invited to renounce: our erring passions, our ideas of God, and our self-made sense of self. Humility is standing in the truth of being. Because we already have what we are looking for—the direct experience of our living awareness—we renounce *what is not* and so, negate nothing.

These teachings about renunciation are tools that the desert elders gave to serious seekers who desired to live life in conscious awareness rather than living heedlessly. These renunciations are described in many classics of spirituality. First, either suddenly or gradually, we awaken and notice that we are going the way of our false self. Then, second, we notice that we are not our thoughts, and so we renounce the thoughts attracting us to return to our former way of life and strive to remove any and all obstacles to our true self. As we see more clearly, we notice that God is not a thought either, so we renounce self-made thoughts of God and let God be

God. Then, finally, we notice that we are not a thought of self, so we renounce our self-made thoughts of self and prefer our true self. This fourth renunciation concerning the thought of the self requires delicate discernment, so that we are not tricked into self-loathing or a version of numbness that leads to inert passivity that would cause us to loop back to our former way of life.

This wisdom can be retrieved from the wisdom of late antiquity, 200–450 C.E. My root teacher of renunciation is St. Benedict (480–547). His most frequently quoted master, other than scripture, was John Cassian (360–420), who wrote the *Institutes* and *Conferences,* a brilliant systematic description of contemplative life. Cassian presents both the theory and practice of contemplative living through his personal contact with the elders living in the Egyptian and Palestinian deserts. This wisdom, along with the gospels, inspired the *Rule of Benedict.*[1]

Beside bringing forward the desert teachings, in this book I present two examples of humility: St. Teresa of Jesus (of Avila) shows us how to renounce our self-made thoughts of God, as in the third renunciation, and St. Thérèse of Lisieux shows us how to renounce our self-made thoughts of self, as in the fourth renunciation. Both of these examples of humility are also teachers of practice through their writings. St. Teresa of Jesus gives us a teaching on the practice of recollection and how to pray appropriately as we wait upon the Lord to come when, where, and how God wants to manifest God to us, as in the third renunciation.

The second example of humility, as in the fourth renunciation, is St. Thérèse of Lisieux. She invites us to practice the Little Way, which is living into the renunciation of self and shifting toward sacrifice. Paradoxically, her way of spiritual childhood is the way to profound maturity. Her own experience of growing up was sudden, but we can undergo this maturation gradually through the wholesome practice of the Little Way. When self no longer dominates and we feel a desire to sacrifice, we know it, and this renunciation is "full of grace"; our humility becomes a way of life, like that of Mary who hastened to visit and assist her pregnant cousin Elizabeth.

The book's final section is a sharing of ten indicators of humility as listed in the *Institutes* of John Cassian. It seems that whether we are monastics or contemplatives in the world we can behold the beauty of humility—that sacred art of simplicity fashioned in the soul. In these ten indicators of humility, I hope to capture the living tradition of these elders that invites us to consider what humility would look like if we were to live it today.

The appendix of this book has a generous listing of scripture quotes for each of the eight thoughts to enable the reader to return to the sources that the elders used. I have kept footnotes to a minimum and hope that the readers will use their Bible as the main source for further study and reflection. The way the elders prayed the scriptures is known as *lectio divina,* and we would do well not only to strive to imitate their words of wisdom but also to use the same process that they used to immerse themselves in "The Way." *Lectio divina* is the art of reading sacred text as prayer.

Lectio divina is a prayer form that engages the heart with the inspired text. The text engages the reader at the level of the spiritual senses, using the literal plain sense as a starting point and an ever-present ground of reality. Revelation courses through consciousness as a stream wends in between hills and valleys, lifting up layer after layer of meaning and significance. From time to time the reader encounters the holy and rests in stillness before returning to ordinary awareness with a sense of presence and mystery. *Lectio divina* becomes a habitual way of contemplative seeing, hearing, feeling, smelling, and knowing that we are known.

This book makes use of two metaphors: the journey and the river. The image of a journey is an attractive symbol that captures the notion of the ancient quest and connects us with the likes of Abraham, Jesus, Anthony of the Desert, Mary of the Visitation, and historic heroes available as teachers in all cultures. The journey implies a calling, a vocation, and a response in faith. This journey has two simultaneous dimensions: one is external, which is seen by our families and friends; and the other is internal, known by the heart in secret but in harmony with the universe.

The image of a river provides a graphic and poetic metaphor for grasping the twin dynamics of the journey, inner and outer, and also helps us understand the four renunciations. Our life above the river is what people see: the external life, marked with refusing to follow Christ. When we are initiated through baptism, the sacred waters are briefly parted and we plunge in deeply, only to be lifted above those same waters and swept into the Christian way of life. We vow to live the first renunciation of our former way of life, to live in communion with all the faithful who treasure the gospel and extend their hands in charity, especially mindful of the poor. But there is another dimension, a deeper immersion; our life below the river is known only by the heart. This interior orientation moves us into more profound depths of renunciation where we surrender our passions, our self-made thoughts of God, and even our self-made thoughts of self.

And so the pathway of the real spiritual journey is underneath the surface of the river. This hidden way of life is what is actually going on in the interior thoughts and feelings. From above the river, no one can see any other person's motivations, which are nourished from beneath the river surface where there is rich, energetic life.

A pilgrimage observed from above the river can seem like any other trip: fly to Lhasa, stay in the Tibetan Quarter hotels for tourists, travel by jeep to the monasteries with their restored temples and stupas, eat Tibetan food, meet interesting people, take pictures, write a diary, and then fly home. But underneath the river surface there is an inner journey full of openness to profound encounters, real austerities, ceaseless prayer, mystical moments of beauty, break-through insights, and profound awe. We return home from a journey below the surface of the river forever transformed.

This book is for pilgrims who dare to travel in the depths of the river. Since it is a hidden journey that has been navigated by many who have gone before us, we learn from our elders. Some of us have an intense attraction to live as they did: consciously committed to the way that brings us to humility. In following the teachings on the four renunciations, we realize humility.

So enjoy this book. Move through it slowly in a leisurely way conducive to *lectio divina*.[2] The whole constitutes a system, so read the entire book, then give yourself years to live into these teachings. God is patient, gentle, meek, and humble of heart. We are created in God's image and are invited to live in God's likeness.

1

First Renunciation
Former Way of Life

When I was assigned to East-West dialogue, I witnessed the significance of initiation rituals. Each faith tradition has rites that "make" a disciple of a guru *(dīksa)*, or begin training under a Zen master (take refuge in the Buddha), or undergo the pilgrimage *(hajj)* to Mecca. In these rituals there is power in the doing; but in reflecting on the formulae, the text of required questions and responses, the gestures and exchange of symbols, one can understand what is actually happening. What follows in this chapter on the first renunciation is a summary of our Catholic baptismal ritual. The initiation ritual asks the candidate to renounce his or her former way of life and take up the new life as a Christian. What happens in ritual time takes a lifetime to accomplish. This is the work of the other three renunciations. The baptismal ritual bestows power and grace in the name of our Lord, Jesus Christ.

Though many of us were infants and others spoke for us, we underwent an irrevocable transition. We were plunged into the saving waters that are a sacramental stream of grace in the Christian community and were raised up transformed. We were lifted up, as it were, out of whatever is not the wholesome, generative, and healing life flow of being we call God, and set on a journey below the surface of the river that will bring us to paradise.

Christians believe that the sacrament of baptism is both the sign and reality of rebirth into new life, an initiation that commits us to specific obligations to foster and nurture our new way of being alive. The initiation ritual of a Christian is a baptism with water.[3] This initiation is instructive for our study about humility since baptism is a transmission into living wherein Jesus is alive in us as individuals and into the Cosmic Christ. In the ritual we find many teachings. Also in the ritual we undergo an actual transmission quickened each year on Holy Saturday at the Easter Vigil. Rituals engineer the whole of life in sacred and symbolic moments.[4]

First, the water is blessed, the Holy Spirit is called down to quicken the waters with special mystical powers, saints are invoked in a litany so that our ancestors in the faith witness and join in the celebration. The prayers used in the blessing of the water are instructive. We are reminded of how creation was a gift from God and that life was breathed into all matter. Salvation history is handed on through storytelling and mythic events. We remember that the flood in Noah's time covered the world because of sin. By God's saving power the water was diminished, and there was a new start of a faith-filled generation. Many years later our forbearers were saved again through miraculous parting of the waters of the Red Sea. Descendants were again saved by the baptismal ceremony John presided over using the waters of the Jordan River where Jesus himself underwent baptism and was anointed by the Spirit. This same Jesus poured out his life on the cross. We are baptized into the same Spirit that anointed Jesus.

Then the priest puts his hand in the water and blesses it. He prays that this water does for us being initiated today what was done to Jesus. We are anointed in his name. We ritually die to sin and receive the living grace of newness of life.

In the second part of the ritual, the priest asks the person being baptized, or the one speaking for him or her should the baptism be done for an infant, to renounce sin. The word *sin* has many meanings. In the rite of baptism rejecting sin or being freed from sin means shifting one's entire life toward God and away from evil and ignorance. The person affirms that this is their resolve.

With each affirmation, we renounce our former way of life in exchange for a new way of graced living in Christ Jesus. After the baptismal ritual, the candidate makes the promises to reject sin, reject the attraction of evil, and refuse to be mastered by sin. Satan as the personification of evil is renounced. And in place of sin is an affirmation to avoid evil and do good.

These affirmations are followed by a profession of faith as stated in the creed, then there is an immersion in the water or a pouring of the water using these words: "_____ (name), I baptize you in the name of the Father, and of the Son, and of the Holy Spirit."

The rite continues with an anointing that confirms the person into membership. Then the ritual continues with the clothing of a baptismal garment. And, finally, the newly baptized is given a lighted candle:

> Christ has enlightened you.
> Walk always as children of the light
> And keep the flame of faith alive in your hearts.
> When the Lord comes, may you go out to meet him
> With all the saints in the heavenly kingdom.

In this foundational renunciation signified by baptism, we surrender our false self, generated by our egocentric desires. Since sin is living heedlessly, harming others or ourselves, we renounce these patterns of ignorance and sin by choosing a better way for ourselves and others. Furthermore, we enter into a process of critical discernment not just between good and evil, but regarding the hierarchy of goods. In other words, I renounce not just what may be harmful, but also what even may be objectively good in itself, but not good for me. The phrase "former way of life" describes attachment to our family, property as possession, status linked to employment, rank in society, educational, racial, or gender entitlements, and any over-identification with what I do. These attachments dull our zeal and give us a kind of numbness born of unconsciousness toward our real life and the lives of others.

Since baptism is usually a ritual for bringing a newborn into the Christian family, you might ask how an infant can have a former way of life. The ritual of baptism is a transmission into a mode of consciousness that transforms one into a state of wakefulness. This might take the whole of childhood and even extend into adulthood. In this sense, our "former way of life" is the time before we "woke up." It also refers to a kind of obscure mode of awareness that seems to be our human lot, unless we are engaged in some spiritual process or program of true "awakening."

When do we awaken? In a sense, there is a part in each of us that has always "known," in a spiritual sense, but then as life and time progress, this dimension of our being grows numb. Some children are keenly awake, and in childhood there seems to be an innocence that is a paradoxical mode of knowing. But over time this knowing dims. The Greek theologians talk about the *nous*—meaning both heart and mind—being darkened. In this dim stage our heart/mind lives dimly, too. Relationships and resources are squandered; we neither recognize nor spontaneously choose the good. In this "former way of life," there is a vague awareness of living below the level of our true self, trapped in a life dedicated to selfishness, sin, and the pursuit of things that are apparently good but in actuality are not contributing to one's spiritual life.

When one renounces one's "former way of life," this life unto death is replaced by an apostolic way of love. We imitate Christ Jesus, as the early disciples are described as doing in the Acts of the Apostles. We see the early Christian community living by new motives, sharing goods in common, mindful of the poor, keeping the gospel as sacred and a way to restore the original order of creation, fulfilling civic duties, and striving to live justly according to the words and deeds of Jesus. Like these early ancestors on the Christian way, we renounce our former way of life precisely to live the gospel life.

There is a simple test for what this former way of life was for each of us: Was this way of acting the way I acted before I was a nun? Or a spouse? Or a parent? At the time of this writing, I am 62 years old and can look back and remember the way I was before I entered religious life, before I made final vows, before I was prioress, before I had the practice of ceaseless prayer, and so on. The simple truth is that there is grace that moves us from light to light. But this conversion is difficult to sustain. We get pulled down. We sometimes are ignorant of the good. We are inclined toward evil and are thin on resolve. We tend to get weighed down by our human condition—whether the primordial sin of the earliest generations, or the sin of our immediate generation, or our own personal sins. The way out is to return to those baptismal waters and take the plunge again—this time diving deeply into the saving river. Each time we take the plunge and rise again, we commit ourselves to the contemplative or interior way of life. In a sense, taking up the spiritual journey is to live beneath the surface and to stay immersed in those baptismal waters with Christ Jesus and then to rise with him above the water and live as he did.

Every Christian is asked to renew his or her baptismal promises annually at the Easter Vigil. Many times there are newcomers to the faith being baptized in the same ceremony. The Easter Vigil of Holy Saturday is the most sacred moment of the church year. There are the forty days of Lent by way of preparation. All Christians are called to affirm that they are renouncing their former way of life and taking up the new life in Christ.

During the Easter Vigil, the priest introduces the renewal of baptismal promises with the following words, while the people hold a lighted candle, like the one given at their baptism. He says,

> Dear Friends,
> Through the paschal mystery
> We have been buried with Christ in baptism,
> So that we may rise with him to newness of life.
> Now that we have completed our Lenten observance,
> Let us renew the promises we made in baptism,
> When we rejected Satan and his works
> And promised to serve God faithfully in his holy catholic church.[5]

Then, the priest continues with the affirmations that mirror the questions asked of those receiving baptism. The rite concludes with a profession of faith, the creed, and the usual eucharistic liturgy.

In the monastery we sustain this first renunciation to change from our former way of life by promising to live the monastic way of life. *Conversatio morum* is the life-long labor to actualize the fundamental renunciation of baptism by a daily dedication to change our habits and patterns of living: to shift from being generated by the ego, or self-constructed self, to being generated by the Spirit of Christ that became the intentional source of our existence in the rite of baptism. This commitment to *conversatio morum* is supported by a whole monastic culture, established to aid the monk in the work of dying to the "former way of life" and coming alive to the new way of life in Christ. The structures and community of the monastic way of life, therefore, provide a rich and enveloping context for contemplative living. Most spiritual seekers, however, have a contemplative way of life without the explicit forms of a monastery. In whatever vocation we have, whether that of a householder or a monastic, the spiritual journey cannot proceed solely above the surface of the river. We must delve below the surface in order to sustain the visible forms of our way of live, whether monastic or domestic. More explicitly, the first renunciation that frees us to live the Christian way of life necessarily leads to the other three renunciations of the spiritual journey. To these we will turn now.

The external journey above the river is to do good and avoid evil. The spiritual journey starts with this plunge into the unseen, the interior life.

2

Second Renunciation

Thoughts of Former Way of Life

To renounce our thoughts and the habits of our former way of life is difficult. The second renunciation is about the mind/heart that remembers and attracts me to my former way of life. The thoughts and feelings from that way of life (sometimes called "the world") cluster around the classic eight thoughts: food, sex, things, anger, dejection, acedia, vainglory, and pride. While leaving the city and going to the desert could remove the physical proximity of things, relationships, and attachments to lifestyle, status, and reputation, the early desert mothers and fathers found, to their surprise, that these same allurements awaited them in the desert. They discovered that they continued to desire God, but there was a drag underneath their consciousness. So they sought a way that, with effort and practice, they could be liberated by the grace of God.

Therefore, the second renunciation is about renouncing the thoughts and feelings of my former way of life for the sake of retaining my awareness and abiding consciousness of God. This is what we mean by a contemplative way of life. There are many ways that different faith traditions name this heart's desire. As Christians, we say that we are created good, very good, and that we are in relationship with God, that our heart and mind are one with God. However, our experience of God is dim and only vaguely or episodically felt. It is only when our thoughts and feelings are stilled that we remember God. To *remember* is a technical word in our tradition. It means to return, like a magnet, to the original imprint of God within us.

God's presence springs up and this consciousness of God becomes a felt abiding. Then afflictions rise again and we forget that consciousness, even though we know in faith that God is here.

So what can we do? The desert elders taught that we must renounce those thoughts and feelings that lead to afflictions and that stand in the way of the direct experience of knowing God. And they taught that, because the flip side of these afflictions is *theoria* or the direct experience of God, the nitty-gritty effort of renouncing them is done in the inner chamber of our heart.

Here are some of their teachings:

- We are not our thoughts/feelings.
- Thoughts come, thoughts go.
- If we do not accompany rising thoughts/feelings with another thought/feeling, these little vapors dissipate like gas in the atmosphere.

Centerg pr

We can watch our thoughts and notice them at their earliest stage of rising. If we catch them early, often, and gently, they lose the power to hook us into desires and passions that offer us temptation. When we consent, we get hooked back into our former way of life. If we act on recurring thoughts that rise and offer invitations, we can get trapped into compulsive actions that can become patterns of behaviors and, ultimately, of captivity.

We can anticipate and correct these interior patterns by praxis—right efforts to follow the subtle promptings of the Holy Spirit. Praxis offers us four options of things to do when thoughts and feelings rise in us:

1. To combat them directly, being aware and directing our thoughts/feelings away from the content offered
2. To simply replace the thought/feeling with another thought/feeling such as the Jesus Prayer

3. To simply watch thoughts/feelings
4. To do good for another selflessly

The thoughts cluster into three categories: afflictions of the body, the mind, and the soul. The thoughts/feelings of the body are food, sex, and things; of the mind, anger and dejection; and of the soul, the afflictions of acedia (sickness of the soul infected by torpor), vainglory, and pride.

Praxis provides us methods to discipline and direct the heart/mind toward a contemplative way of life. A few traditional contemplative practices include the practice of *lectio divina*, remaining in the cell, doing manual labor, practicing ceaseless prayer, sharing a common table, sharing common things, sharing a community of faith, and manifesting our thoughts to a wise elder.

When our thoughts/feelings are stilled, we push away obstacles and become the receptacle for Christ consciousness. When ceaseless prayer replaces abiding mindlessness, then Presence rises.

> According to the desert elders once the voices of the inner person have been conquered and the mind has been established in tranquility it will be possible to enjoy unceasing prayer. "For . . . when the thoughts of the mind have been seized by this purity and have been refashioned from earthly dullness to the likeness of the spiritual and the angelic, whatever they take in, whatever they reflect upon and whatever they do will be most pure and sincere prayer."[6]

The teachings of the eight thoughts contain the antidote to our afflictions. In these afflictions we find the path to holiness and humility. Therefore, the renunciation of the eight thoughts is the second renunciation.

Let us consider each of the eight thoughts that can become afflictions. This is sometimes called the purgative way, since it purges us from the desire to return to our former way of life. Though the afflictions are simply thoughts or desires, they can easily lead us to fully return to the time before we were mindful, aware, and conscious of God's presence in our soul.

Afflictions of the Body

Food

Consuming food is a universal experience. We desire food and drink, and that desire recurs frequently as a strong urge to eat or drink. In monastic training the thought of food is the first tool to be used because it is an everyday thought. In everyone food thoughts rise and seek to be satisfied through eating and drinking.

According to the teachings of Evagrius on the concept of *logismoi*, thoughts have a common process from beginning to end.[7] When a seeker goes to a desert elder, the elder attends to the movements of the heart and mind of the seeker, examining the suggestions there, the inner promptings. If an impulse or inner prompting has already developed into an outward deed, into consent of the will, it will be too late simply to manifest this to the director. Then one must go to a confessor and resolve not to wait so long next time.

The elders identified different moments of temptation. First, there is the suggestion, which is free from blame. Next follows the coupling (an inner dialogue with the suggestion or temptation), then the struggle against it, which may end either with victory or with consent and sin. When repeated, such acts produce a passion and in the end a terrible captivity of the soul, which is no longer able to shake the yoke of the Evil One.

The proper object of revelation of thoughts is the first stage of this process: the suggestion. I must crush the serpent's head as soon as it rises. The entire strategy includes: vigilance, watchfulness of thoughts, guarding the mind, prayer, especially the invocation of the name of Jesus, and so forth.

John Climacus in his famous *The Ladder of Divine Assent* reports the distinctions that were already hallowed long before his time (579–649 C.E.).

The progression of thoughts is as follows:

1. Provocation—thoughts rising, simply rising
2. Coupling with dialogue—an interactive phase
3. Assent—moving along the possibility
4. Captivity—fascination with the idea of doing it
5. Struggle—and finally, perhaps, consent
6. Passion—the full pattern linked into the yoke of evil

Food and/or drink can be a teacher in one's interior life. The thought can rise and be satisfied (we can eat or drink), or it can be laid aside by using one of the four methods that dismantle thoughts:

1. To combat them directly. Being aware, direct your thoughts/ feelings away from the content offered to the mind.
2. To simply replace the thought/feeling with another thought/ feeling such as the Jesus Prayer.
3. To simply watch. With awareness, thoughts/feelings simply are not able to gather the energy required to hook the self.
4. To do an apostolic action. To do good for another acts toward God, and thoughts/feelings follow when charity is done selflessly. Thoughts are stilled, and goodness overrides the human propensity toward sin.

Particularly helpful to the food thought (also helpful for the thoughts about things, though not about sex or anger, as we shall see later) is the notion that the royal road is to take the middle way. We need food and drink to be strong for the journey. But there are three criteria that can keep us in the center. We need to eat enough, but not too much (quantity). We need nourishment to sustain us, but not so dense that the rich foods or drink diminish our ability to work or get proper rest (quality). We need to eat often enough to fuel our energy sources, but not so often that we overwork our digestive system (frequency). It is just as harmful to eat too little as too much, to eat too low on the food chain as too high, or to eat too seldom as too often. The middle way is the diet of steady, sustained energy.

Eating according to the middle way not only sustains us for contemplative living but is the first step in learning the secrets of the interior life. We have already seen the cycle a thought goes through before it becomes an action or a pattern of behavior. Noticing the food thought as it rises is an amazing tool for discernment. Little thoughts, or *logismoi*, rise and cluster into feelings and desires. The more we watch the more we can catch the thought before it becomes attached to a feeling, when it is simply a freestanding vapor. At that point it simply comes and goes quickly unaccompanied by another thought.

When we see the thought coming, and even see an accompanying thought, that is an invitation to consent to the first thought and to entertain it as a fantasy (as in eating mentally . . . tasting the early morning coffee and fresh baked scone). We can back down the thought, or sort out the stages of the thought and pause between the invitation and the consent. This pause makes all the difference. In this pause we can consent or consent not. Notice the language of "consenting not" rather than "not consenting." The secret of this early tradition is to *unthink* rather than think. This theme will reoccur often in this book, so if it isn't clear, just let it be an option for now. But let me try to explain:

I see the thought of coffee rising in my mind's eye.
I feel the warmth of the cup in my hands and smell the fresh aroma.
I'm being offered in my mind the invitation to taste my memory of coffee earlier this morning.

Now if I unthink at this point, I shift away from the next thought, which would be a fantasy about drinking the coffee. Unthinking is sorting out my thoughts (*diakrisis*). I am not my cup of coffee. I am not my thought of my cup of coffee. I am free to choose or not to choose the cup of coffee. I am free to choose or not to choose consenting to drink the coffee. I am free to think another thought rather than the thought of the cup of coffee. While the thought rises, I can notice it and unthink it as well as think it. If I unthink any of the three thoughts listed above—and I may have to repeat it several times—the original thought about coffee recedes from my consciousness.

This unthinking process has wonderful benefits. There's a mind at ease that can either drink or not drink the coffee, and can eat either brown bread or a scone, with equal poise. The mind at peace is the beginning of *apatheia*, dispassion. Notice that this is not apathy, but the full conscious involvement of living from the center. While smelling, sipping my coffee, I taste the real brown bread before me and not the fantasy of the fresh scone that I had yesterday. The present moment is more satisfying than a memory.

This sorting goes beyond having a simple thought into seeing three categories in that thought: quantity, quality, and frequency. How much is too much or too little? What is too poor in food value or too rich in calories or fat? How often must I eat and how often is not enough to sustain my energy level? This sorting is the beginning of discernment. The middle way trains not only the mind but also the body. The body gets used to this happy medium.

This sorting is the task of the individual. No one knows me from the inside the way I know myself. I know when I've eaten too much or too little. I know which foods are too dense for my digestion and interfere with the conversion of food to fuel. I know the rhythm of meals that seems to give me sustained productivity both mentally and physically. Although a strict interpretation of discernment is that it is a gift of the Holy Spirit, and one cannot discern one's own thoughts because it is the very thoughts themselves that need discerning, to sort out my thoughts and discipline my appetite is my job.

The training goes on then to the practice of fasting according to the middle way, that is, not too much, not too little, not too high, not too low, not too often, not too infrequently. This kind of fasting is recommended as a lifestyle. It is not penitential. It is simply natural.

After their early desert training, some monastics practiced austerities that involved severe fasting from eating or drinking. This is a later tradition that overshadowed the earlier healthy and moderate way of eating. Penitential fasting took on extremes to accomplish purification, using food to heighten body consciousness rather than God consciousness. Purification fasting and extreme austerities are discouraged, if not forbidden, in a monastery. If done at all, one must get permission from the superior so that it is done under supervision and in the service of contemplation, not for unhealthy self-abuse. For most of us the moderate, middle way of fasting is difficult enough and more than enough training for purification and discipline.

There are two exceptions, however, to the moderate fasting of the middle way. The first one is feasting. When it's time to feast, no one should be fasting. Feasting is always eating much, often, and rich. It's a time to celebrate the graciousness of God's gifts to us. It's time to enjoy the end time now, because we have great hope in tomorrow's beneficence. There will be enough and we need not resort to patterns of scarcity. It's festival time, a time of grace (*chairos*), not linear time (*chronos*). This event now is to celebrate life in all its living. Feasting is abandonment to the mystery!

The other exception is hospitality. We lay aside our patterns of middle-way eating by serving the needs of the guest first and then taking care of ourselves. We might eat more or less, depending on how we provide for them. We might eat again, so they do not have a meal alone. We might serve the best and join them in our finest treats, or we might silently serve them what we had intended to eat for ourselves. All rules are in the service of the Guest who is God. Hospitality again is a way of discernment, using the other's needs rather than our own as the criteria for eating and drinking.

There are a few other considerations about food as training for discernment, and I will mention three here.

To abstain consistently from certain foods or drink is a worthy practice. As Christians we have a choice to drink wine during gatherings of believers. Observant Muslims, Buddhists, and Hindus refrain from all alcohol. Christians eat meat. Muslims and Jews do not eat pork, and Hindus and Buddhists refrain from meats (with the exception of Tibetans who had so few grain and fruit options living at such a high altitude). Again, like the food discipline described previously, fasting is not about food so much as about fasting from *attachment* to thoughts of food. Abstaining is not about prohibiting certain foods or drink so much as using these options as an object of training, just as an athlete uses resistance tools to strengthen muscles and bones.

The Christian teaching is that all food and drink is good in moderation. The thought of food helps us to be nourished but can also be a skillful means to knowing our thoughts and teaching us how to discern to live wisely.

Some persons have addictions and/or chemical imbalances that require continuous vigilance so that recovery is ever in progress. Once more, the wise person knows herself and replaces denial with vigilance (*nepsis*). To watch and pray behooves all of us. We need God and cannot sustain our resolve to be in God's presence simply by willing it. If we in any way consider ourselves above the law, life is precarious. Humility is the abiding disposition that accepts life as it is and lives it consciously, fully embracing its burdens and its gifts.

Sex

The second thought that rises is about sex. Sometimes it comes so fast and with such force that it seems to arrive as a full-blown passion without moving through the discrete process like the thought about food presented in the previous section.

Sex desires rise for everyone, but this universal experience is particularly sharp when one leaves family and relationships to become a monastic. That vocation requires a new way of life, and our former way of life rises with raw and renewed vigor. The sex desire is strong, fast, unrelenting, and seductive. This deeply felt feeling has enormous power, force, and vitality from puberty till death. If not well ordered, sex energies can destroy, actually denying us life. There's no question about the goodness and potentiality for health and wholeness, as well as holiness, that the sexual energies serve. The teachings from the desert tradition are explicit and helpful for the married and monastics alike. No one is called to suppress sexual energy, but we are all called to be transformed through our sexual energies.

Three degrees of sexual activity help distinguish aspects of our vocation (calling us from deep inside our inner dispositions):

Continence is simply no-sex for one reason or another.[8] Maybe we do not have a mate, or the inclination or necessary time and health for sexual partnership. To be continent means simply living life without sexual activity. This stage of no-sex can be for a time, as when we are a student, or between having babies, or perhaps even during seasons of one's relationship. To be continent most of the time is not really virtue, but it is simply the way it is now. It is indifference in actual behavior, and it can be mindless in preference and intention. This is why no-sex isn't the way to live. One must dedicate one's sexual life according to calling. There is a huge difference between continence and celibacy.

Celibacy is ordering sexual habits in accordance with one's chosen state in life.[9] Married partners are celibate with all persons except their mate. Monastics are celibate with all persons but are also continent for a lifetime, in order to be faithful to their celibate vocation. Celibacy is a vow to order one's sexual energies toward God's design and in consonance with one's own true nature. In one way or another, all persons are called to celibacy: to ordering one's choice of sexual activity according to one's choice in life.

Chastity is an interior, not an exterior, virtue. Because we order our sexual desires by interior asceticism, to be chaste is to be in control of our interior thoughts and desires. If we are celibate, chastity requires us to practice the method of unthinking in order to redirect our sexual inclinations to our vocation of celibacy. If I am married, I cultivate loving, interior thoughts toward my mate; if I am a monastic, I notice my sexual fantasies and offset them with my practice of prayer and apostolic service.

Both married and monastic contemplatives have a profound realization that mortality is a fact: I'm going to die. And I am going to die alone. Naked we come into the world and naked we leave this realm. This "going alone," unaccompanied by any other person, has a double impact: sometimes a stirring of truth, which may even be exhilarating, that I alone can and will make that natural passage—or sometimes a dread of this inevitable solitary activity. But in this sense all and each of us are called to be celibate. We live and die alone. Before we die, some are called to marry and others are called to be intentionally continent, as having no sexual partner. All are called to be happy and to thrive.

Sex, in and of itself, is life-giving, but it also can become an affliction that is an obstacle to contemplative living. There are many teachings that govern sexual afflictions. Here are a few that have contemporary considerations.

Sexual thoughts, fantasies, dreams, and physical attractions need not surprise us. We are made to mate and propagate. We have a wonderful propensity for engagement and social interaction. Full human development requires sexual fulfillment. We were made like this, and it is indeed very good.

But sex requires discipline to achieve satisfaction and for the right reverence of another. This discipline orders our sexual passions in our chosen vocation of celibacy, whether married to another person or monastic. Chaste thoughts are our right effort to direct our physical drives to sensitivity to others and to ourselves.

It's good to be aware of and to be committed to one's vocation so that we can cultivate appropriate habits. There is a big difference among being open and actively seeking a sexual relationship, being married and committed to one partner, and being a vowed monastic.

Therefore, discernment of one's calling is essential. After our vocation is chosen, we must practice celibacy and chastity according to
that vocation. Celibacy is not a state in life; it's a way of being in the
world, a practice.

The practice of celibacy is according to one's vocation. Chastity
is the responsibility to guard our heart and watch our thoughts so
that they are appropriate toward our celibate calling. We know our
resolve to carry out our commitment to our particular calling. We
prevent people, places, or things that offend that calling from enter-
ing into our hearts. Thoughts rise and we either redirect them or we
unthink them, as we described earlier. We can prevent abuse of our
heart by avoiding those occasions when we are sexually stimulated.
If we put ourselves in the midst of intense sexual energy, we'll feel
it, and eventually we'll have to deal with it. So why sow seeds we
have to root out? Guard the heart and keep it from temptation.

We watch thoughts rise that are in contradiction to our chosen
choice of marriage or being a vowed religious. As we watch these
thoughts, we see where they came from. This practice has practical
implications for our habits of watching television, social meetings
with friends, clothes, recreational reading, movies and plays, music,
dance, and other forms of entertainment. We become aware of the
type of humor we enjoy, the physical touch and emotional ex-
changes we cultivate. We anticipate our sensual involvements and
make choices that are consistent with our celibate vocation. Sometimes we have a full-blown affliction, being overwhelmingly attracted to stolen affections. We desire another's spouse, a totally satisfying sexual experience with a stranger or an acquaintance, or even
a fantasy. As we watch these thoughts, we can re-order our priorities
of time, associations, and social commitments. These normal inclinations are recognized and can be backed out of our consciousness
with humor and graciousness. To do otherwise is "just not who
I am."

There is a link between well-ordered eating and drinking and
well-ordered sexual relationships. Overeating and drinking diminishes judgment, as does overworking and over scheduling our time.

If we live a reactive life, we deprive ourselves of the poise born of the stillness where sexual energies are kept at some distance for wise discernment.

There is also a connection between physical exercise and sexual energy. Physical exercise through manual labor or sustained body movement—in walking or strength training—doesn't offset sexual energy, but a steady walk diminishes the level of intensity. Normal life forces range between rest and exertion.

There's a surprising interaction of energy that flows between bodies in proximity. Someone "in love" can affect another person in the same room. The heat or field of energy is felt within a physical radius. It is a common tragic story that one person feeling the love of another can mistakenly imagine that the other person is "in love" with them, when in fact the love is directed toward someone else. The object of love and the proximity of the body can involve two different persons. Sexual energy is like the heat of the sun. You feel it.

There's an interesting correlation between judgments—harsh critical thoughts—and one's own sexual desires. We tend to become what we judge most wrong in another. The seeds of that very same affliction in us are projected on another, or we can say that we see it in another and we condemn it—yet we water the same affliction in ourselves so it springs up with a vengeance.

Conversely, it is compassion toward others that best assists us in ordering our own passions. We somehow embrace what we see is our condition mirrored in others. We implement our own programs and enter with enough maturity to fail and get up again with gratitude for God's mercy in our daunting lifelong process toward integration. We see others no less tempted than ourselves and understand how difficult lifelong fidelity can be.

We watch our dreams at night and notice whether our sexual dreams involve people we know or whether they are images arising from stories we've been told. Are they memories from our past or are they the hidden desires that remain a distant longing? Simply noticing seems to make all the difference. Explicit sexual night dreams can indicate that our sexual energy is in need of conscious effort to return to our celibate commitment. Some need to work harder at having quality sex, and others need to work harder on our valued commitment to no-sex.

Our daydreams are equally seductive. It will become more evident as you continue to read this book that free-falling fantasy runs counter to spiritual consciousness. Daydreams can and do contribute to the chain of acting out. A rampant current addiction is to pornography on the Internet. To cultivate a *virtual* sex life contradicts our vocation and causes disintegration and breakdown in our *actual* relationships.

What about self-sex? Is it appropriate and healthy to release sexual tensions? The release obtained by masturbation is natural and certainly not sinful. However, the alert conscious mind directs its energies toward its inner calling and its outer responsibilities. Therefore, to cultivate a virtual sex life contradicts our vocation to reality.

Sex thoughts have their own life cycle and can oppose integration. To be married to a fantasy spouse is not healthy. Life and all its consequences are best played out in actuality. Sex thoughts, more than other afflictions, can be not only seductive but also deceiving. In the darkness of inner solitude, one can set up a whole inner life that is a lie. At first we know the lie simply as a fanciful tale intended to provide an escape from the harshness of reality. If we entertain these tricks, however, our mind can seduce us into thinking the fantasy is real and we can become people of the lie. Sex thoughts can serve to divide the truth and confuse our heart. It is one thing to lie to others while we know in our heart that we are double, but it is another thing to lie to ourselves and eventually become the lie.

A practice intended to lead us toward the truth, regardless of the consequences for our heart's integration, is "manifestation of thoughts." This manifestation brings into the light all of our thoughts, especially thoughts that are afflictions. This practice goes back to St. Anthony, St. Benedict, St. John Cassian, and St. John Climacus. The theory is that our thoughts loop around and hook us. We can watch them and see the points of contact, of invitation, and of consent of the will. Some thoughts, of course, are slicker and more insidious and catch us before we catch them. To deal with these thoughts we need help. One of the best helps is to lay out our thoughts to a wise elder who can

1. give us the opportunity for honesty and speaking the truth, and
2. help us to notice when we are getting hooked and are taking action that is against our best self.

The process of the manifestation of thoughts goes like this: Each day the person observing this discipline writes down the recurring thoughts that keep rising over and over again. This list is the beginning of the old practice of the examination of conscience. If one writes down the earliest awareness of the rising thought, one can see the cycle and redirect the energies. Having done this, the person shares these thoughts with a wise elder who receives them—simply receives them and watches them from his or her vantage point without judgment or scolding. If an inspired word rises in the elder, then that word is shared; if not, the manifestation of consciousness is received and the elder simply gives the practitioner a blessing.

The process is routine, and sometimes the practitioner brings the same list over and over again. Eventually the affliction subsides if it is not fed with worry, aggravation, condemnation, or stimulation. The traditional wisdom seems to say that the only kind of thoughts the practitioner is not to share is the memories of sins that have already been forgiven. Going over them again and again, continuing to give room to them, is to risk depression and despair about God's mercy.

What about homosexuality? I believe the same teaching is applicable to same-gender sex as to opposite-gender sex. It has been my experience that gay and lesbian contemplative practitioners can enjoy peace and satisfaction from the practice of celibacy. Can gay persons be celibate married and celibate monastic? The answer seems to lie in accepting the way God has made us and affirming the consequences of the adult responsibilities that ensue. The teachings from the desert tradition are critical of those who judge the sexual afflictions of others, yet they extol friends who exhibit the honesty to will and refuse the same things. Some argue that to reach out to the gay community is to condone rather than condemn their sexual behavior. Why should any condition prevent pastoral love and respect? Why do we fear? Perhaps, instead, we need to apologize for our neglect.

Although we are clearly women or men, there is a benefit to transcending (not repressing) our gender consciousness as an end in itself, in order to see ourselves and others. We are humans who happen to be male or happen to be female. In our innermost heart, to love is to let mystery be spacious and pervasive, even undifferentiated in one-ness. We transcend our two-ness as a way to unity and in service of union. If we cannot, we miss the other *and* ourselves.

Monastic celibacy is a lifetime choice of no-sex with any other. Why would anyone do that? What benefit is the life of a celibate monk or nun to the individual, to culture, to the cosmos? Most persons are called to celibate marriages, to cleave to a partner and have a lifetime together. That's the norm. Some people choose not to do this for one reason or another, but it may not be for the sake of monastic celibacy. The reasons for celibacy in the monastic way of life are not purely functional or to increase efficiency. To get more done, even for the apostolate, is not worthy of a calling. To spend less money because you are without family and possessions is not the object of a vow. The rationale for non-married celibacy continues: To be on call to a bishop seems unworthy of both the authority and the member. To have more time for contemplation is not a compelling reason not to have a spouse and children.

Is monastic celibacy, therefore, a random choice? Or is it a rare calling, as in a miracle, that God invites someone into a direct relationship by-passing the sexual order? Or is celibacy outmoded? Did it once make sense but is now even harmful, rather than being a higher calling or a good?

What is the reason for celibacy? It makes sense that celibacy in marriage is healthy for children and household stability. It is essential for one's spouse to be one's only partner with no other living in the same heart space. It makes sense that chastity of mind be valued, since it's duplicitous to have a celibate marriage and yet have another spouse in one's heart space held deceitfully from the eye of one's mate. Having an e-mail partner is an increasingly common way for fantasy and reality to collide when spouses discover that their partner has been pursuing a "virtual" relationship by e-mail. When this hidden relationship is brought out into the open, it can be explosively destructive. So, what rationale can we give for celibate monastic or celibate married life?

The three reasons that all mystical religions give for celibacy are:

1. We search for the unity of our being, reducing multiplicity and fragmentation. The only other is the ultimate Other.

2. We transmute our sexual energies. Sexual energy, when sublimated through meditation or through service, shifts us into higher states of consciousness. Since their sexual energies are transmuted, note that married partners who are celibate also use their sexual energies to achieve higher states of consciousness.

3. We accept the direct path to the Divine. A nun or a monk is seen as the spouse of Christ, and this espousal is qualitatively different from gender-to-gender sexual relationships. This is mystical union between beings. Again, nothing prevents married couples from also experiencing such a spousal relationship with Christ. This experience brooks no contradiction. It's a both/and experience.

If these are the reasons for celibacy, does it make a difference whether one is married or monastic? This transmutation of sexual energy in service of contemplation is really the deepest, most fundamental purpose for each of us whether married or monastic.[10] It goes back to our calling, our vocation. Some of us are called by God to be celibate in marriage, to be celibate in the monastery or beyond it. This old teaching on states of life requires discernment. We discover our vocation with prayer and by listening to our deepest self. Each of us knows that we know and are known. To be chaste is to be the same in the day as in the night.

Things

Things are holy. Things are for our use in order to be and to become. Things are tools, instruments and devices to use for something else. Things are neither essentially possessions nor are they idols. Things are seductive; they seem to follow, then can begin to lead. Things are simply things. We are not our things just as we are not our thoughts. All the teachings on thoughts can be applied to things, which are projections of our thoughts. Things provide great tools for discernment. We can sort them: not too many, not too few, not too expensive, not too cheap; we should not be too frequent or too infrequent in acquiring or ridding ourselves of things. Things do not satisfy us and seem to spawn the desire for more things. The more we have, the more we want. The better we have, the better we want, and the more often we shop the more often we increase our shopping. Things seem to have a need-generating life of their own: We . . .

  need a new computer
  need to upgrade software
  need to put on a virus protection
  need to have a back-up system
  need to have a tech support system
  need to have a workstation
  need to have upgraded electrical accessibility
  need to have more time to work on my computer
  need to have an assistant
  need to have a security alarm system
  need to code my private data
  need to have more in-service training on computer
  need a new digital camera

need to have a printer that's better for photography
need an iPod
need a new office chair that fits my back better
need special computer glasses to ease eyestrain
need to have a part-time job to pay for my new computer
need to have a new car to commute to my second job
need to wear classier clothes for my new job
need to have an office that has a better view
need to have an office with its own entrance and exit for privacy
   and convenience
need to hire my own tech assistant to stay current
need to have surround sound for music as I work . . .

It seems ludicrous, but it's all too real. Things beget the need for more things. How do we sort them? We start with our vocation. Usually what we are doing now is our vocation. If we are married with a family, then we are a householder. If we are a nun in a monastic community, we are a monastic. Householders have things in service of their family and civic community. Monastics renounce things and then obtain the use of things through the permission of the superior under whom they live in obedience. Both are called not to possess, but to have things for their use.

The teaching on renunciation of things is rich and applicable to us today: We reverence things as precious and to be used with respect and gentleness. Things are good in themselves, and we need to honor all things, all creation. Things, however, are objects of human persons, and we misuse them when we exchange the Christ consciousness abiding in our hearts for the "things" we want to acquire, distribute, use, or possess. If things possess us, we become "thing" conscious rather than Christ conscious. We become obsessed with the things we must have to be happy. These desires shift respect and the right order of things into greed and grasping for more. We take more than we need, more than we can use, store, or keep in quality condition. We hoard, we have contempt for others who have less, and we enjoy status and exclusivity.

The myth of the Garden of Eden was about things that were plentiful, lush, and well ordered. The test was to be content with what was given. Our primordial ancestors accepted no limits, boundaries, or control and wanted to be equal to the Creator rather than the enjoyers of creation. We are put to that same test over and over again in our own little earth gardens. And rather than graciously receiving things and returning them to our Creator with gratitude, our actions cause us to be cast out of that garden. We join our own personal sin to the primordial sin of our ancestors.

We restore that garden with the return of things to their proper place. Householders use as their guide the questions of how many things, and of what quality, they need to make their dwelling or business a healthy, holy place to live. Monastics seek permission to use things in service of their assigned obedience. We take the things given in obedience and reverse our tendency to grasp them, hold each thing lightly, gently, for as long as it is given for my use, then freely offer it to another for his or her use.

Things tend to divide. "My profession requires more things; my family was deprived so I need to compensate; my taste is so discriminating that I need to satisfy my eye for quality." All this may be, but things never satisfy these deeper longings. Having enough is more satisfying than being satiated. It's better to have less, lower quality, and older things than to divide the community, destroying its harmony and peace. Things serve life; life does not serve things.

Our addiction to things increases when we desire the things that another has. We want them. We believe that their right to have them is not as strong as our need to have them. Jealousy is insidious. It begins as admiration for the good taste of another. Then greed makes me envision myself as having those things. Then I fantasize that I deserve them at any cost and could steal them or harm those who have what I want. The disorder of jealousy can rob my judgment of any balance and proportion, as the thing becomes an icon of my happiness. After a while the thing is not even the object of desire. I am willing to harm the one who has what I want. If that happens, I take on the affliction of envy—wanting to destroy the very being of another. Ultimately, this can lead to the tragedy of murder. A simple thing becomes my identity, and I no longer live with anyone who competes with me.

Beauty deserves special consideration. Right-ordered things do not have to be sterile, stark, and without artistic and contemplative qualities. Our sufficiency must always include the essentially good, true, and beautiful things in nature, art, music, dance, poetry, mathematics, drama, crafts, architecture, interior design, graphic arts, and literature. To return to a garden without things of beauty would profane the temple.

The affliction of things is like the affliction about food. The food thought is not about food. It's about the thought of food. The affliction of things is not about things; it's about the thought of things. When we lay aside our lust and greed and appreciate our heart's desire, we make well-ordered decisions about food and things.

Things only become idols when they are internalized as a condition for happiness. Greed is being insatiable about the quantity, quality, or frequency of the acquisition and distribution of things. If we are greedy, things become seductive, and the tricky manipulation and distortion of our motivation begins. "This is for the poor," I tell myself as I acquire something better and give my cast-offs to the poor. Or I tell myself that compensating myself enhances my psychological well-being, or that I deserve this, or that only I can appreciate this quality, and it's a waste to share it with those with a less cultivated taste than mine. I can extend the benefits of these goods, I think, but first I must have more, better, even the best to keep up my reputation. If I'm deprived, I get angry and depressed. I must prevent myself having a bad mood.

When manifesting thoughts to an elder and the affliction is things, it's good to notice not only the thing I desire but also why I desire it. Also, when watching thoughts rise it's good to identify the moment when the grasping inclination becomes consent. The mind shifts from I would like, to what I want, to what I need, to what I must have, to what I *cannot* do without, to how I am going to obtain it, to—I have got it! Does this remind you of advertising?

Sometimes things come in an insidious guise. The need to get things done follows the same sequence: I'd like to do this, I want to get this done, I need to do this, I must do this, I'd never forgive myself if I passed up the opportunity to do this, I cannot *"not"* do this, I now see how I can do this. Does this remind you of strategic planning?

The monastic discerns with the help of the superior. Do householders have a way to discern? Our family, neighborhood, spouse, relatives, job, and talents provide the ordinary will of God for us. We are called to where we are at this time and place, and the grace of God for us is stored in that moment and place. We need only be open, receptive, and willing to respond to the call of duty. When there is a question about whether to do this or that, we stop and ask for confirming signs to reveal God's direction, then the fruits of the Holy Spirit follow.

Does living consciously mean unceasing inner mental torture? No, just the opposite. A mind that watches and knows its patterns and inclinations can be at rest, and the watcher can choose this or that with confidence and poise.

It seems that after this early period of watching or keeping vigil (*nepsis*), the spirituality of the desert was replaced by the more scholastic analysis about the good of the action and about willing the good. In this transition, the watcher became an instrument of moral good and bad, and the emphasis was on the will rather than on the first glimpse of the thoughts rising. When we first notice thoughts rising, we can often avoid the battle with the will. We become more astute and wise about our subtle thoughts, feelings, emotions, desires, and inclinations. We smile. The brute force of the will has no power over our heart's desire.

Things are things. All creation is good. We need not master nor dominate either things or ourselves as users of things. We need not clothe our desires with illusions of possessing things, but act as stewards of creation. We see the monastic value of obedience as a wise means of discerning how much we need, how many is enough. We see that obedience requires our motivation to be examined. Why do I need this thing? Why now and why for me? Obedience shines light on the whole. Do others need it more? Can I share? Is it in service of the community?

The poor provide an opportunity for discernment. In the light of my needs, when do I have enough? All major religions have an imperative to give to the poor, to give without return, and to give no matter what I might think I'm entitled to. No one, not even monastics with vows, can say that they have no obligation to the poor. Monastics are to live in such a simple way that the community can offer goods to the poor. Monastics renounce giving to the poor in their own name, but must live in such a way that the poor are served through their apostolic outreach. No contemplative is dispensed from this apostolic love. We live in common and we serve the poor. Those with less should benefit from our common life.

To cause others to suffer, even through negligence, is harmful to ourselves. We are called to relieve the lot of the poor, to ease their troubles. Through the merits of Christ Jesus we participate in redemptive suffering. The use of things gives us a chance to understand this and to practice wise use of things so that by living simply others can simply live.

You see that there is a great leap of logic, from sublimating my suffering as a way to recognize its value to me to substituting my suffering for the suffering of another. We can only intuit this through mystical senses, not through logical thinking. This teaching is not about things in and of themselves, but about the flow of things as mediums of good, of power, of energy, and of grace. In the Christian tradition there's no loathing of things, just as there's no loathing of food and sex. We receive them graciously. Things and grace become interchangeable.

Things are mediums of our desires. Things provide a skillful means for obedience, for renunciation of our insatiable desires, and for enabling us to be autonomous and self-sufficient. Things are sacraments of caring and compassion. The Garden of Earth returns to the myth of the Garden of Eden.

Afflictions of the Mind

Anger

When we do not get what we want, feelings of anger rise. Anger, according to St. Basil, is the single biggest detriment to the spiritual life. Rage shifts our consciousness toward the self, the ego-self. Discernment is impeded. Thoughts cluster and harden the heart. *Diakrisis* or sorting is not possible. Anger, however, can be a skillful means to notice one's attachments, projections, judgments, and critical harshness toward others, provided the anger is owned as "my program," caused by my view. Note the distinction: anger is "my view of the behavior of others." We can view others' behaviors without anger. We can see wrongdoing and extend compassion, as in our former way of life we used to mete out anger.

Is anger ever justified? The teaching is clear. No cause, no matter how harmful, justifies anger. In the spiritual life righteous anger has two fundamental flaws identified in these two questions about anger: Whose righteousness has been offended? And is it right that I set myself as judge over another? Anger sets up a violent reaction to violence, and the cycle continues escalating toward hate and hostility.

To have been harmed once by another's sinfulness is bad enough. To be harmed twice happens when I turn around and retaliate. I'm harmed, so I will harm another. The proper response is quite different. I'm harmed, so I will not harm another, no matter how tempting that is. I develop emotional poise and with God's grace respond with loving-kindness and compassion.

No matter how much harm is done to me, anger is not the preferred response. This difficult but mature response is the opposite of suppression. It is a choice of action that requires full self-conscious awareness and true self-expression.

Anger takes on subtle forms of retaliation like kicking the door or driving aggressively or yelling at the dog. Anger is anger and displaced anger continues the cycle of violence. Peace is possible, but difficult. Sometimes there's no apparent cause of my anger. We are just in a bad mood.

Since anger diminishes spiritual insight, it's worth the trouble to practice patience. Elders who have anger afflictions forfeit the privilege of being spiritual directors because—no matter how much their anger is disguised—an angry adult gives anger rather than wisdom to a sincere seeker. Anger shows itself in cursing and swearing, harsh words about another, deprecating comments about authority, the conditions of the place, the presentation of the food, the flow of the traffic, or the way someone dresses, speaks, carries her body, or sits in a chair.

Anger begets anger and the cycle of violence gathers more violence. Violence soon becomes undifferentiated, and there's a culture of hate and retaliation toward the enemy. If I am angry, good becomes simply defending my principles and bad becomes anticipating how I can make threats and preemptive strikes against those I fear. Anger is the early child of murder and war. The lie about anger is that it would actually feel good and be good to harm another. The truth is that we must do no harm to another; we must love others, even our enemy. I cannot hurt another without harming myself.

An angry reaction is to use words that harm another. Calumny is to speak about another and harm their good name. It might be a truthful fact, but not necessary for me to promulgate. Slander is to actually speak and promote lies about another and testify false things about another as if they were true. Everyone deserves a good name, and for us to devalue another has an irrevocable and damaging effect on that person's social well-being. Calumny and slander, however, most harm me because I falsely put myself above the other either in judgment or in vanity. My own being is tarnished. If I do this, I am not to be trusted. If I am not trustworthy, I forfeit the honor of bearing witness.

Anger is so common in our culture that it's difficult to see it as an affliction. It is an obstacle to one's well-being, equanimity, and peace of mind. Anger disturbs the mind, divides the heart, confuses the intellect, and poisons the body. Anger is toxic. Anger makes us sick, says the Dalai Lama. Many studies show the enormous toll anger takes in the form of undue stress on the body and mind.

We can feel anger, however, and resist going up the chain of rage. The alternative to anger is to take action when the heart is at peace and the mind has discerned the right action to take. We ourselves do not know what to do in the face of evil. We must wait and be willing to respond without contributing to the evil, or we become instruments of evil ourselves.

Anger is sly and devious. It has many faces, many methods, and can even be full of humor and a classy style. A put-down or imitation of another's weakness is entertaining at first, but it has the same effect as directly damning another. Depreciating someone else has its source in anger and is nourished by innuendo and gestures of contempt. Even silence can be co-opted by anger.

We need not get caught in anger's grasp. If we become skillful at noticing anger rising, we can feel the emotion of anger, but we do not have to feed its stings and whips. This takes practice. The tool is guard of the heart. We know ourselves. We refrain from people, places, things, and conditions that water the seeds of our anger, which might be wounds from childhood or traces of former traumas. We catch anger before anger catches us.

I'm writing this in Ireland. It rains here almost every day and usually more than once a day. The rain doesn't surprise me, but what does surprise me is my own comments about the rain. I say, "What a shame that it's so damp and cold from January through December." That it's damp and cold is a fact. I need to learn from the Irish how to dress warmly, keep dry, and anticipate the cold before it penetrates the bones. The tea is wonderful, and so are the steaming soups and roaring fires. The wool sweaters breathe with the body heat, and the air is easy to breathe, as the water is clean and tasty. So it rains and so it is cold and so I need not be angry. It is as it is. The rain and the dampness can be my teacher.

Although no one can make us feel angry, we can absorb emotions from another if we are not mindful. An angry teacher unknowingly solicits anger from students, and it takes a skillful teacher to withstand a roomful of angry adolescents. We feel the emotional field that is emanating from another person. And love is as contagious as anger.

Anger disqualifies us from being practitioners of the spiritual life. We *cannot* pray when we are angry. At first, we are just angry, and then we are angry about being angry. Prayer is unthinking, sitting before God in humble adoration. Anger is disputing with God and sitting in defiance of what is.

We can lift up our anger as we'd lift up any affliction and suffering and ask for God's mercy. We can open our hearts before our community members and marriage partners and speak our troubles. We can seek their advice and listen to how we might have brought this anger upon us—as in "it's really our problem." We can ask for forgiveness and for the grace to start over in our relationships. We can ask for help to go into treatment for our anger problems, as for any other addiction.

Anger is an energy sourced in the body. It is sometimes fed by fatigue or by overeating or overdrinking. In my experience anger can be modulated by attention to diet, exercise, and getting enough sleep.

Anger is preempted when we go out of our way to anticipate our angry reaction by offering forgiveness first. This is a difficult thing to do, but it's easy to be ready—at least in one's own heart—to offer peace and reconciliation. This must be done sensitively, however, so that the other doesn't react negatively to our forgiveness, and we could be rubbing salt on the wound and offering, rather than a sincere greeting, a hollow greeting of peace. We must pray for our enemies.

Resentment rises when we've nursed anger over and over, and our emotion is convoluted into a dark cloud of hostility toward the whole situation as well as everyone and everything involved. Then we resent the resentment and on it goes. When we give in to anger and resentment, it becomes habitual and easier to transfer to this person and to that, to this situation and to that. We become blind to our own complicity in the situation and even close windows of opportunity for the other to ask for our pardon.

Anger has an intoxicating effect and feeds upon itself. Anger can feel good because it has an affinity with power. To embody power and absorb the excitement of can-do, will-do, have-done actions is heady. Anger addictions compulsively attract violence. The other is the victim—conquered. The appetite for blood is insatiable for the predator. It takes more and more to satisfy. Rage becomes the way I am when I do not get my way. And I will do it my way. Submission is weakness. No wonder St. Basil says that anger is the biggest obstacle to the spiritual life.

The Our Father is said several times a day in the monastery for a good reason. There is no more ongoing conversion than to forgive, to ask to be forgiven, and to anticipate tomorrow's "done unto me" and readiness to forgive no matter what the hurt. Sometimes anger has a chemical cause that shortens our fuse. We need to acknowledge our part, no matter how small, and after careful diagnosis ask for help through anger management programs or drug therapy. Alcohol or self-medication through over-the-counter drugs usually exacerbates the condition.

To see anger and to return compassion is difficult. Once we gain experience, we can see that the sooner we practice compassion rather than anger, the quicker the anger affliction subsides. There's another pattern that is more difficult to overcome. When hardship comes, or we've been hurt, though we can accept it at first with practice, a deep layer of resentment rises that engineers a "getting even" or retaliation syndrome.

I can get a "no" from my superior and accept it with a few rounds of inner resistance, but perhaps then I will find some hostility that re-asserts my dominance. It might take the form of deprecating my superior or getting my way about something else. That thing itself might not be necessary, but it makes me feel that I'm back in control. Since I was controlled at one point, when something comes along that I can control, I do so. The cycle spins. It's a subtle cycle of violence.

The teachings from the desert tradition are clear and concise. The monk ought not be angry. No matter how small or how large the hurt done to you, you must forgive and not be angry. The anger will not go away if the one who causes it leaves or if the monk goes off to live in a cave by himself. He'll get angry at a dog or a pen or a stick.

Anger is the affliction of the monastic that is the most harmful to prayer. One *cannot* pray when angry. Anger makes one blind, and we *cannot* see the truth of the situation. One is blind with a little anger as with a lot of anger. We *cannot* see and therefore are disqualified from being a spiritual director. When someone comes to an elder who is angry, she receives anger rather than a word that comes from a discerning heart. Anger prevents discernment. Anger makes you sick. You can go mad (psychotic) in rage. The clear eyes, bright face, and radiating smile are replaced by anger. A grim and repelling countenance repulses even animals.

The antidote to anger is patience. To be silent and wait till the heart is stilled and the right action is prompted by the Holy Spirit is the way out of the affliction of anger. We must never let the sun go down on our anger. We are to forgive. We must also let the other person change. I have had the experience that the other person repented and I resented it. I wanted a reason to stay angry, and I wanted to be the forgiving one and not have to admit the other's virtue. To be meek and humble of heart is a lifetime grace inviting effort.

Dejection

We continue the teaching about the second renunciation with the affliction of thoughts of dejection that become depression. Here there is a shift in tone. There is softness and a different voice. The afflictions of food, sex, things, and anger seem to be directed to the monastic who is striving to seek God and finds these afflictions to be obstacles in the way. The affliction of dejection is different. The teaching is directed more to the community than to the victim of the affliction. Here we see compassion and a delicate understanding of the depressed one.

Dejection, when not redirected, leads to depression, but from where do the dejected thoughts/feelings/emotions come? Six causes are traditionally given, a teaching dating back to about the year 300 C.E. There are also six recommendations that we can extract from these teachings.

If we cultivate a pattern of despondent thoughts and deprecative self-talk, a negative mood naturally follows. But why do we put ourselves down or even let others put us down? In the previous afflictions there is no analysis of the source of the affliction. For instance, with the anger thought, no matter what the source, the treatment is the same: forgiveness of the other and patience. But in the teaching on dejection, the source dictates the treatment. Dejection can lead to sin, according to Thomas Merton.

> There is a sin of sadness. Sometimes instead of trying to react against sadness, we submit passively to it saying, "it is a cross—God wants us to feel that way." No, God does not want us to submit to the sadness that eats the heart out of our virtues and of our interior life. This is a sin. It is a great self-deception to submit to this sadness and feel virtuous over our self-pity. . . . Sadness in the spiritual life comes from preferring what is destructive and negative, and refusing to take positive steps to be constructively good. It is . . . a cult of "dolorism" or suffering for its own sake, etc., etc. Above all, then, we must avoid a false and destructive spirituality. Just as moths make a garment totally useless, so sadness ruins our spiritual life. If we are to build a spiritual temple for the Holy Ghost, we must not use worm-eaten beams and timbers.[11]

If the dejection is caused by sin, then one must repent, ask for forgiveness, and make amends. Sin has consequences. We cannot strive after truth, right relationships, and integrity while leading a double life heedless of morality. Sin splits our attention, divides our heart, and dices our soul. We become confused, dizzy with "what-ifs," rationalizations that do not satisfy the mind's propensity for wholeness.

If the dejection is caused by harm done to us by our parents, family, culture, or current situation, then we must accept the fact that harm hurts and that we have incurred the burden of another's sin and heedlessness. This kind of realization requires us to face the trauma and seek help to stabilize our mind. We must not say it's okay, or that it didn't happen, or that it didn't hurt, because it did happen and continues to hurt.

The way out of this form of dejection is to let the hurt in all its forms pass without commentary, such as "I deserved it" or "my parents were the meanest" or "if only my brother had rescued me." The incidents simply happened and have caused me harm, and because of this harm I've suffered. I'm neither worse than others, nor better for having this affliction. I am simply suffering the consequences of the actions of others who are afflicted and have wounded me in the cycle of violence. I am human and have experienced this particular suffering. So, the way out of this kind of suffering, of dejection that is caused by harm, is forgiveness and full recognition, awareness, and steadfastness in the face of past painfulness that is still living in my present. Making sense of my own suffering goes a long way toward removing its sting.

Dejected thoughts can also be caused by existential dread. This is not a condition limited to a few artists and sensitive souls. Many adolescents have no language to describe this condition but feel this existential dread. We are called into being and given life, breath, and form. However, there's a deep drag of "not wanting to be" that accompanies many people at some level of existence. This resistance takes the form of depression and even sometimes the choice to commit suicide, because "to be" wasn't my idea anyway.

This resentment—of having no choice in the matter—has to be resolved by a fundamental choice "to be" and "to become." But before we in full consciousness make that choice, there may be a felt, existential resistance to being in relationship with other beings. Eventually, though the sad person may not even understand how the right choice gets negotiated because the problem is so deep down, one comes to accept the fundamental option to live, including all the consequences and burdens of life. To live becomes my choice and not just something that happens to me. With that choice comes an inner power of self-determination. Once that is done, the depression is replaced with exhilaration about life and all its participatory activities.

Existential dread may also go beyond the individual self; it is dread of being a part of the whole, dread of being a "thou" in relationship with others. This dread looks around at the group or culture one is born into and sees its faults, causing depression, because the collectivity that one belongs to, not by choice, is extending evil in your name.

Depression is depression no matter what the cause. The good news is that dread that causes depression can be relieved even if the cause for the dread *cannot* be removed. Being human is difficult, and we undergo suffering oftentimes not of our own doing. But we can have compassion where once we had depression. At some level we can fundamentally accept what is as well as what is beyond our control. Depression is our resistance to what is and a defiance that shows itself in the need and will to control what is beyond nature and grace. Just because we are created in the image and likeness of God doesn't lift us out of the human condition.

Another source of depression is the realization that I do not like the way my life has turned out. I look back and regret choices, or feel the sting of wrongdoing that I did, or am ashamed of my past. Or I see the burden of my past really narrowing down my opportunities now. I must live here with this group of people and with the experience and training that my obligations incur. Or I see the narrowing down of options for the future that are consequences of my present constrictions. I will not be a famous composer, or a scientist making that medical breakthrough, or the owner of that business, or the mother of those children, or the writer of that book. Choices bite and have particularity. Midlife crisis is about this kind of depression. If I live in the future or the past, I miss the grace of the present moment.

And finally, there's a depression that comes from sources unknown. Monks and nuns all through the ages have committed suicide in their cells. Even in the earliest literature there is a description of a kind of depression that is sudden, without warning, or from no cause that can be detected. Now we would probably say that the person suffered from a chemical imbalance or a personality disorder.

Today there is medication to treat the symptoms and give amazing relief that sometimes is enough to rest the brain so that it restores itself. Some patients must be humble enough to remain on the medication, with all its side effects, for a lifetime. Currently, even with severely depressed clients, there is a good deal of research pointing to the benefit of non-drug-induced meditation as beneficial to training the mind to equanimity.

The teaching on dejection that leads to depression talks *about* the dejected person, not *to* them. They are not available to themselves, let alone to the teacher's admonitions. What is evident though is that the elders are to keep the despondent person within the flow of the community. The depressed person is to be swept along and held in prayers, at the common table, and in the common life. Depression only worsens in isolation.

The affliction of depression affects children, adolescents, adults, and the elderly and can be felt intensely even in the midst of success, in healthy communities, in work situations, or in family life. One's goodness is simply not felt, and darkness eclipses one's well-being. There is usually not a sequence of thoughts, such as a story that prompts anger. Depression is a mood disorder, an undifferentiated darkness and thickness that feels either numb or as if one is alienated from all that is linked to meaning and/or personal intimacy.

The suffering of dejection goes beyond the physical realm, and the teaching about it begs the caring community to stay close to those bearing the weight of this burden. A compassionate community can lift the dejected one out of this protracted abyss. Supported by such a community, many persons move beyond depression and never return to its iron grip. As they look back, they are assured of mercy and mystery. Mercy is universally and always available, and mystery is experienced in the deepest realm of our being.

The six causes for dejection are sin, harm, individual existential dread, collective existential dread, anxiety that comes from choices one makes that narrow options, and physical deficits that are chemical or genetic in nature. There are six doors to healing dejection: 1. confession, 2. forgiving others, 3. choosing life, 4. right thinking that is neither inflation nor deflation, 5. making peace with life choices, and 6. taking prescribed medication. It is likely that all types of depression can benefit from many or all of the above remedies.

There is probably a seventh cause of depression that I've watched in some of my older nuns. About a year or two before their death they seem to undergo a deep darkness of mood. They seem to face the ultimate fear that maybe there's nothing beyond.

When one nun was dying, I walked down to St. Francis Hospital on Holy Saturday morning to pray lauds with her. She said she didn't think there was anything beyond. "And Easter?" I asked. She shook her head, closed her eyes, and went into a coma-sleep. I never saw her again with her eyes open and alert. Looking back on the life I had known with her, I realize that she had many signs of chronic depression. I remember that Easter morning bringing her in prayer to our Eucharist and festive singing. Was she just in a dark night? Did she die in despair? Could I have done anything to lift her mind? Hopefully, my own faith and the faith of my community overshadowed hers. Did she feel our faith in her last earthly moments?

I'm confident in God's mercy that she's well and happy in the beyond. Because of the affliction of depression, any light, life, and faith were hidden from her. Even if her inner experience was darkness, death, and unbelief, imagine how surprising it must have been to her when love overshadowed her memory of earthly life and all was well! My personal belief is that she is going to be full of light when I meet her in the next life.

I like to think that in this seventh cause of depression, when our being passes through death, before we turn to new life, there's an amazing transformation. The body dies, but the soul lives. The cycles of birth, life, death, and new life continue to rise. Could depression be the foreplay of this surprise?

All the afflictions have benefits. As we've seen, the food thought teaches discernment, the sex desire defines our vocation, things can provide skillful ways to be obedient, anger teaches patience, and dejection is an experience of mystery. We have three more afflictions to look at: acedia, vainglory, and pride. There is a system among these afflictions, as you'll see when we continue through the next three teachings. Humility is what lies on the far side of the afflictions, but this comes later in our story.

Afflictions of the Soul

Acedia

Acedia is an affliction of the soul. Laziness is sloth of the body. Listlessness is a mind without starch or discipline. Acedia is a soul sickness. This toxic weariness puts the soul to sleep. I give up. At its endstage acedia makes me live life heedlessly without paying attention to the spiritual journey. Acedia is more than a mid-life crisis of depression. Acedia is a profound temptation to forget striving and simply give in to whatever feels opportune. All surrender is abdicated and hopelessness prevails instead.

The symptoms are profound boredom and irritation toward current conditions. Discontent sets in about everyone and everything. The monastery is dull, unwholesome, substandard, and even harmful for physical and psychological health. Leadership is unenlightened and the rules are not laws I am to keep since, at this stage of my insight and training, I'm above the law. I know better and am ready to be the superior, or perhaps even start my own community.

At the very least I'm the only one who knows how to live monastic life and no one listens to me. No one knows how much I'm suffering! Depreciative name-calling usually follows, as acedia picks up where depression leaves off. A wife and mother escapes in doing more volunteer work at church and neglects the home saying no one appreciates her, anyway. Or the husband takes on another "wife," his business, and moves up the corporate ladder, drifting further away from the obligations of married commitment and spending more and more time at the office and away on trips or off with the "boys." What makes this acedia and not just dejection is that the intention is to get someplace else because there's no return to the ego in one's prior commitments.

Acedia becomes a lifestyle for those who didn't negotiate their mid-life crisis. The noonday devil becomes my mate. The sun stops and long days and sleepless nights or the torpor of both day and night do not ease my fatigue but aggravate my disposition. Hostility against everyone and everything dominates me, replacing my early zeal as a novice and the steady life of the vowed monastic. Vows lose their connection to me "as if" someone else made them. The rule serves only to annoy rather than invite. Most rules are obsolete. If only I were the superior, I'd change this observance to optional preferences. This rule stifles my creativity. I should leave this place—it's an obstacle to my growth and a detriment to my health. I will die if I stay. And so the inner dialogue continues. Or the householder says that I need to invigorate my soul with another lover. There's even a twist of conscience that I'd be more alive for my married partner if I had outside relationships to quicken my passions.

Acedia can last for years, perhaps even a decade or two. It's so uncommon that the word in English *cannot* be found in any spell checker. Would it ever be confessed as a sin? Is it preventable and is there consent to it, as in any other sin, or is it a condition that all serious seekers must pass through?

The teachings from the monastic elders are unanimous that the affliction of acedia is a temptation that when accepted and acted upon is harmful to both the practitioner and the community. There are moments of consent, but there are also antidotes of prevention and of treatment. It is so harmful because, while the earlier affliction of depression might lead to suicide, acedia can lead to "soulicide." The soul is forsaken. Instead of renouncing obstacles to my soul's growth in love, I renounce my soul and live as if I have no inner consciousness that forms and informs my life. Acedia begets a conscious choice to go back to sleep and stay there, numb and unresponsive. From there it's a very small step to renege on previous renunciations and live totally for myself.

Acedia is equally harmful to the community. The tepid monk spends his time poisoning others. This is the same monk who formerly spent hours and hours in *lectio divina* and manual labor. Now this monk travels from here to there indiscriminately and brings back the toxicity of the world, infecting the imagination of others who might be worn down by their own weakness of resolve as the years go on in the monastic way of life. The acedic monk now is bored and leaves his cell whenever he can, viewing all observances of silence as antiquated and harmful to his social self. He sows seeds of discontent about leadership and about the way the monastic life is lived or not lived.

He promotes himself as the next superior, even speaks of founding a new community and openly recruits a separatist group. In short, the acedic monastic divides the community and pulls weaker members into comfortable patterns of laxity. The vacation *from* the monastery soon becomes a vacation *in* the monastery. Vacation replaces vocation. Endstage acedia is a vacuum of apathy where once there was zeal.

So the symptoms are boredom, murmuring, restlessness, social contamination, promotion of self-interest especially as leader, absence from choir, cessation of interior practices of *lectio divina*, fasting, silence, chastity, and obedience. The monk takes a leave of absence from real monastic life while keeping the minimal forms of wearing the habit and living in the monastery.

This is so harmful to the group that St. Benedict recommends excommunication. This monk is to be isolated and not allowed to share the common table, common prayer, and common work. A wise elder (*senpecta*) is sent to minister to him lest he get dejected, but hopefully so that he will see his precariousness and return to his vocation. The community is instructed to ignore this erring one, as it is not good for him to have access to opportunities that undermine the zeal of the community. This affliction of acedia is contagious and care must be taken that the whole community doesn't follow in the same energy field.

Is there a parallel excommunication for married partners undergoing acedia? Perhaps there is a need for separation. First, separate from other couples that encourage marriage arrangements that are fragile in commitment. Then, there is separating oneself from each other for the sake of discernment, sorting thoughts and feelings. To flee to another relationship confuses the situation and harms another person. Excommunication is for the purpose of not harming the other. Most relationships, whether marital or vowed monastic, must endure times of diminished affect and original zeal patiently. We know that our hearts wane, but we also can return to, and even surpass, the passion of our original "being in love."

It takes a while for leadership to recognize the acedic member, since this seems normal in our culture. But once this affliction has been detected, action must be taken before the whole community becomes infected. I've seen entire communities caught in these chronic acedic patterns. No one knows exactly what's wrong, but the virtuous or zealous newcomer is jeered, and any new leader that takes on the crowd is met with disdain. If depression is the affliction that is unable to receive the kindness of others, acedia is the affliction that numbs our spiritual senses.

John Climacus speaks extensively about a monastery set up for wayward monks where they have a wise elder and there is a culture of repentance. We might be able to prevent hardening of hearts if each of our monasteries fostered honest, real day-to-day reconciliation. Some Trappistine nuns have a daily opportunity for self-disclosure before sitting down for a common meal. The erring sister simply reports her misdemeanor. This is respectfully received, then they say grace before the meal with gratitude for all the blessings they have received that day. If we are to forgive before the setting of the sun, we need points of entry to do that in a human, face-to-face way; otherwise, this action can become another rigor of the rule that is not lived in our times.

Not only members of a monastic community have this affliction. We recognize it in parishes, schools, religious communities of apostolic orders or dioceses, health care facilities, and families. The patterns are evident: Zeal is loathed, deprecating talk saturates conversations, and expectations are low. Comfort-seeking replaces mission and self-seeking pleasures replace spiritual practice.

The problem with this affliction is that the soul becomes dead. I am right and everyone else is wrong! The person still goes to all the rituals but feels nothing and routinely zones out. The mind wanders out of its cell of the heart and has no boundaries. A "what if" sequence replaces ceaseless prayer. This disease destroys our effort toward praxis and becomes a steady state of ennui.

Acedia can be a teacher to all of us. The wonderful teachings on the cell, manual labor, compunction, and the gift of tears are stored in the teachings on acedia from the desert elders. Let me review them briefly here.

The cell is a place of refuge throughout the whole of a monk's life.[12]

First, it's the warm sanctuary of solitude for *lectio divina* and an endless search for the deeper meanings of scripture and life.

Secondly, it's a place for sorting out the many conversations that echo long after a visit or a homily, or perhaps a teaching that pricks my consciousness and probes my desires. Relationships are often sought after in social moments, but it's really in the cell that we feel substantial peace and can sort our affections and lifelong friendships. This is done alone, with the self naked to the self. Patterns of bonding, breaking, meeting, greeting, and boundary-setting become clear. This period of living in one's cell is precious and rich.

When acedia sets in, what formerly was comforting and cozy now is cold and sterile. The cell holds no attraction. How I can leave my cell becomes my inner conversation rather than *lectio divina*. I revisit relationships, reputation, fantasy, and memory with great allurement. The cell is now second flight. Once I left the world and came to the monastery. Now, I flee from the cell (and maybe the monastery, too) and go to my heart's desire, perhaps a new profession, a new accomplishment, a new intimacy, or a new geographic place. I reject my cell as a place of refuge and exchange it for travel, comfort, or a mission with huge ego dividends.

A perverse tragedy is to use the cell to escape from myself and from others. Electronic virtual reality with headsets masking silence and e-mail fly-casting in cyberspace can hijack the monastic way of life for our generation if we are not discriminating about when, where, what, and how much we download into our cells.

The cell is prevention and treatment for the affliction of acedia. If the monk's cell is nothing but a bedroom or an entertainment center, the affliction is nourished instead of rooted out. The cell is the monk's place of personal practice, the mirror of the soul. It's hard to exaggerate the necessity of a cell for both monastics and lay contemplatives.

The praxis is to train the mind and the heart. The heart is my sanctuary wherein the Presence is felt either through faith or through fact. This tabernacle in the temple of our own bodies re-starts every day after a night's sleep. We awaken and our ceaseless prayer rises; we become conscious of the day's needs and guard our hearts and watch our thoughts to keep from any obstacle to our heart's desire. We offer all our merit to God's glory and adore the Holy One who created us. We ask for forgiveness, for both deeds done or not done, through a ceaseless disposition of repentance. We leave our cell for work, prayer, and hospitality, then return and close the door on our anxieties, "shoulds," and "woulds," and return to our recollection of the Presence. We keep vigil especially into the night, as we know we are vulnerable and have tendencies toward forgetfulness, unconsciousness, and indifference.

We design the cell in such a way that it is our place of practice. It is simple, uncluttered, and has no alien vibrations that militate against our monastic way of life. Our simple cell is also a quiet place of devotion and beauty. Art, sacred music, calligraphy, crafts, literature, or anything else that contributes to our *lectio divina* has priority in our cell. We are alone and day after day we cultivate the mind (inner praxis) using the cell (outer practice). The cell is the tethering point fixing my heart's desires in the monastery.

In the affliction of acedia, the cell is boring and the temptation is to flee. Our flight is from inner praxis and the practices that dispose one to contemplation. The cell becomes a place of wrestling and resistance when our intoxicating zeal wears off and the active life begins to require the whole of our intention as well as attention. Acedia is a crisis of motivation.

In the affliction of acedia, the warmth and zeal of initial formation cools to hardness of heart. There are no longer cozy feelings, but instead a loathing of the prayers, routine, daily labor, pious homilies, admonitions, liturgical rituals, and customary disciplines. The life that was previously so satisfying now seems crazy. The cell becomes a prison and the monastery a total institution restricting my human development.

The affliction of acedia is most noticeable in the cell because I have no affirmation or return from my inner work. I'm stuck and sick of soul. I no longer desire the contemplative life but to return to my former way of life, above the surface of the river, free from all this inner work. The teaching about the cell is that I should remain in the interior praxis of my cell and let the quiet burn off my need for self-aggrandizement and esteem. The false self *cannot* thrive in the cell. I must die to my false self. The cell becomes a tomb for that self. My cell is the asceticism that can treat my affliction of acedia. I return to my inner work without inner consolation. I am a novice once again.

The work we are assigned in obedience suits our talents and the needs of the community, but the monastic way of life has a priority for manual labor. The primary goal of the work of the monastery is not to get things done or to serve others. The work of the monastery is contemplation. Through contemplation the universe is transformed. The most suitable kind of work is manual labor because it can best harmonize one's inner praxis with external practice of selflessness. The monastic can also be assigned to teaching, nursing, computer work, social services or business, but everyone needs manual labor to do contemplation.

Manual labor is work that is physical, repetitive, never finished, always needing more attention, and something that I can do while my mind is recollected. The most suitable work for a contemplative is hidden and necessary, requiring a low level of skill and never noticed for either praise or blame. It requires little supervision and one can be alone while doing it. Socially, manual labor is in service of the group and is usually interchangeable. I can see my name on a list, see my assignment, and know that someone else can also do it just as well as I.

This kind of work extends the practice of the cell and the praxis of ceaseless prayer. I'm present to the Presence. Doing manual labor is not simply a physical chore, since you can see how it fits into the overall pattern of contemplation.

Some years ago I had a practice of taking an early cup of coffee before an hour of meditation (centering prayer) each morning in my cell. Then there was another shorter period with a small group of nuns in the oratory before morning office. During a period of restlessness of mind and acedia that made my cell a burden, I cut short my hour's meditation and went back down to the kitchen and did the dishes from the night before. More than sixty of us live in this monastery, so there are always three or four racks of dishes ready to be washed. I'd take the manual labor as an opportunity to focus my mind on each dish, each separate operation of the routine job. The Jesus Prayer was the mantra and the dishes got clean.

The second year I did the job I not only did the dishes with ceaseless prayer, but I watched thoughts rising: "There go the novices again—they are all gaining weight because on Sunday night they eat ice cream," or "Those are the leftovers from dinner," or "Sister

Nancy is never here, then leaves her dishes for us to do later," or
Sister Irma has company again and look at all their mess," or "Here
comes Sister Georgia and she never observes morning silence. . . ."

I could see thoughts rising that really were going to take off during the day. I'd watch and refrain from feeding them with more
commentary. When my practice is in great form, I not only watch
my thoughts but I also detect my motivation: "I wonder if they
notice that I'm doing all this? It used to be Sister Dorothy, but now
look how good I am!" Now, I want not only to watch my thoughts
but also to watch how gently I move each dish silently and rever-
ently. The dishes become vessels of the altar—of the altar within my
own heart.

In summary, manual labor gives the contemplative a way to contemplation. With repetitive, physical, and routine tasks the mind is
at ease and can be stilled in the midst of dailiness. Acedia moves out
of the body, and the mind returns to the joy of contemplative practice. It's best if the manual labor is something that does not have a
life of its own, so you do not have to think about it. It's best if it
doesn't have a high profile for success or failure, causing the mind
to fly into dejection or vainglory.

Work is work and there's harmony in it when the dignity it deserves is allowed to thrive naturally. The greatest teaching manual
labor provides a contemplative practice is that there is no separation
between work and prayer. Work is prayer and prayer is work.

The affliction of acedia causes many a monk or a nun to leave the
monastery or a married person to leave a marriage. Neither the cell
nor the marriage bed is a refuge, nor does manual labor satisfy the
ache of a dead heart.

"When did it happen," the fifty-year-old nun asks, "that my vocation went cold and my prayers drifted into forgetfulness and my
mind started this terrific unrest and dissatisfaction?" She goes on to
say, "I used to like holy things. Now I loathe spiritual reading,
books, retreats, and all these senseless prayers and long services. I'm
wasting my time and frankly have lost my stamina. My back bothers
me, so I sit during prayers. I'm reading light, casual authors, do

mostly e-mail and telephone when I have my own time. I sleep a lot and take more sleep when we have retreat days and late rising on weekends. I visit more. We have a table group after morning prayers, and we get our feelings of negativity out. It's always the same nuns who join this table. Sometimes we meet again for four o'clock coffee and talk about how tiring our day has been. If I were the superior, things would be different around here. Sometimes I think this place is actually harmful to my health. I'm thinking I might leave for a couple of years or so. My elderly aunt needs help. I would like a sabbatical from my job. This conversation continues in my mind and with my associates. I've shifted out of the idea of a cell and it's now my bedroom like the one I had before I entered. I have it all set up with everything I need. I do not have time to do manual labor. The younger nuns can do that just as I did during my first twenty years in the monastery. It's good discipline for them, and I've paid my dues."

This affliction of chronic negativity turns mortally serious, and imperceptibly I renounce my inner life of God consciousness and return to my former way of life back to the surface "above the river." My spiritual journey is at risk. My commitment to acedia is to make a choice that the external life and all its living replaces my vocation. I renounce the interior journey that I so eagerly embraced, promising to live from "below the river," seeking God with my whole heart, body, mind, and soul. I leave my monastery or my marriage; or I leave the essence of my commitment and take a leave of absence *in place*. That way I still look like a monk or a married partner, but will not be available, present, or accounted for. I really do not care anymore.

Part of the toxin of acedia is that our dissatisfactions are fuzzy, hazy, and undifferentiated, so no choice is made and we just drift on to the next stage. If we have an acedia affliction, our leave of absence usually has no form, but everyone else knows we have it. Most people leave years before they actually turn in their keys. I knew a nun who was afflicted with acedia and decided to take a "leave of presence" instead of a "leave of absence." What this consisted of was to get a month or two of leave from work or ministry, to turn off e-mail and phone and rein in her mind. Often we go on a vacation and we bring our acedic person to the new climate and environment, get a few days of relaxation, and then return to our commitment with more restlessness and soul fatigue. Taking a vacation-in-place can shock the system into restart.

What is the difference between acedia and burnout? The term *acedia* is used to describe a spiritual affliction of the soul. The will grows cold and powerless to do good or to resist evil. In particular, it is a spiritual distaste for the good connected with charity—so that the will remains inert and does not move itself to avoid the evil opposed to charity, or to do the good that will obtain greater charity. Thus, under the effect of acedia, charity grows cold. Merton says that if we accept this coldness with indifference, then it is a real sin.

What about burnout? It seems that this is the result of overwork and probably a misguided expectation of some kind of return, perhaps praise or compensation. Burnout may be more of an affliction of vainglory than of acedia.

The most significant teaching about the acedia affliction is that one who is cultivating a hard heart has a condition that can't be fixed from the inside. It often takes a blow, a crisis, or a sudden sorrow. Compunction is the word for this event. The blow punctures the heart and there are tears, wholesome sorrow, and a literal falling to the knees in remorse and awareness about one's wrong direction. For those who have had this experience, any description is trite compared to the way it feels and how it literally changes one's heart. There's a moment before and a moment after that awakens one to the precariousness of the situation and the necessity of doing something. Pierced to the heart, that same dead heart bleeds from sorrow. This compunction of heart is a grace and *cannot* be willed, but it can be prayed for. The abiding disposition that remembers the event of compunction is *penthos*. Remembering the way we were shocks us into seeing how at-risk we were in our spiritual life. Ceaseless repentance replaces heedlessness.[13]

It's easy to see how serious the possibility of suicide is when one takes one's own life out of the endstage of dejection. But it is much more serious to commit what I have called "soulicide," when we renounce the spiritual journey and decide that having a hard heart and doing no spiritual practice is who I am and that my vocation is to live for myself.

Compunction is not rare, but the gift of tears that often accompanies it seems to be a rare gift. The morbid sorrow of dejection is replaced by the purity of having experienced being forgiven. Starting over is natural and graced, as full emotional energy flows from within and without. These tears are full of joy, marvel, and awe and the proper emotion is to cry. The teaching is that we may not receive the gift of tears, but we should pray for the grace of compunction. The memory of our moment of compunction keeps our hearts soft, and we do not return to our previous ways of dead living.

How can we tell the difference between morbid sadness and wholesome sorrow?

Morbid sadness:

1. is impatient (cannot stand the humiliation of the self)
2. is hard
3. is full of rancor (resentment, spirit of revenge, and bitterness)
4. is full of fruitless sorrow and despair, meriting punishment
5. robs us of all energy to work and do penance
6. is irrational, making it impossible to pray
7. destroys all the fruits of prayer and of the Holy Spirit.

Wholesome sorrow:

1. produces true penance and firm stability in the interior life
2. is obedient
3. is affable (cheerful with others, not angry at them)
4. is humble (not based on rage against the self)
5. is meek, sweet, and patient, impregnated with the charity of God

6. seeks hard and painful things for the body and the soul out of love

7. is full of joy and hope, and contains within itself all the fruits of the Holy Spirit. (Gal. 5)[14]

Acedia does pass, thank God, through the gift of compunction. It can be prevented by remaining in my cell doing *lectio divina* and by doing manual labor accompanied by praxis of the mind. When my mind has developed this natural habit, I am happy to be in my cell, but I am also qualified to leave my cell, since humility dwells in my heart no matter where my body is.

If one doesn't negotiate the affliction of acedia, it may seem to pass, but if that happens the ego takes on a new level of control. The next two afflictions, vainglory and pride, are tenacious especially for the one who has a hard heart and has moved back above the river, using skills gained in contemplative practice to serve the false self and to manipulate others into serving them.

Vainglory

Vainglory is an infection of one's zeal. If we do not negotiate acedia and experience the therapeutic event of compunction, we are ripe for the affliction of vainglory. The restless person leaves the cell and takes flight into the world rather than from the world. Fear of one's own false, self-constructed programs is the only way you can detect vainglory. Vainglory often means doing all the right things, but for the wrong reason. Vain means empty or directed toward the self, and glory is the name for God's abiding presence. So, to be vain is to take glory to the self and not to give glory to God. Vainglory is an affliction of the spiritually proficient. If we are not tempted by the left hand of gluttony, lust, greed, anger, dejection, or acedia, we are still not enlightened; we are vulnerable to the affliction of "making it." It's an affliction of the righteous.

Again, these afflictions are about the spiritual journey. What's insidious about vainglory is that we are using the spiritual journey for our own aggrandizement and glorying in being a spiritual teacher, director, writer, confessor, priest, religious, deacon, priest, bishop, superior, or professor. The content of vainglory is theology, scripture, spiritual practice, or liturgy, but the intent is fame, reputation, self-growth, experimentation, competition, or political gain. The person with this affliction renounces the cell and takes on a public persona and religious authority to foster personal motives.

It seems that vanity threads through all the virtues, making it difficult to detect. The vain person may be an eloquent speaker, gifted writer, musician, artist, or even advanced in meditation. This person often has spiritual gifts—may even be able to read hearts, memorize immense amounts of scripture, or meditate in perfect form. But there are ways to discern vainglory in others or ourselves: Failure is a great teacher. If failure breaks me down, it's usually my self-made ego that's in crisis. Without the vainglory affliction, one can make mistakes and even experience complete failure, but still be able to accept this along with all the painfulness of losing face. The same is true for success. If one is a raging success, then praise will be gladly received on the outside and honor and glory will be given to God on the inside. When we see vainglory in others, we should think, "There but for the grace of God go I," and mean it!

Vainglory takes many forms and has stages that slip past even a trained spiritual director. It's the affliction of virtue, using virtue to harm others or to aggrandize the self. It's using spiritual technologies and traditional religious practices as a product. Spiritual consumerism feeds into this pattern. Because there's such a hunger for nourishment for the soul, almost any self-proclaimed prophet can get an audience, a support system, and material benefits. Cassian actually uses the phrase "inebriated by vanity."[15]

Moreover, vainglory can be so insidious that the vain individual really becomes the "person of the lie." At first there's an awareness that I'm really not that good, or that there's so much I've not done to deserve this honor, or if they only knew how many times I've failed and that this is simply random good fortune. But then the affliction of vainglory co-opts the ego and tricks the person into saying, "I guess I *am* the best there is, and that I've earned this. They had better notice or they will regret it."

The person afflicted with vainglory has a perception of self that is completely contrary to that of humility. Vanity means taking one's view of self from the view of others. I live, move, and have my being according to the perception that I think others have of me. Then, as that behavior becomes habitual, I actually believe I know what others think of me and manipulate their responses in my favor. I become insatiable for affirmation, recognition, and attention from the outside. Soon the view I have constructed from others' view of me becomes the view I have of myself. I become my own false self in the light of the false self I've created to get a satisfying response from others. I become addicted not to food, sex, things, but to my image of myself! Narcissism is the endstage of this lack of separation from myself. It is the opposite of the shift from self to sacrifice. Vainglory is a shift from self to ego.

The vain person often does the right thing, so the harm done to others is imperceptible. The harm done to others is that they are duped into thinking that they are getting sound teachings and pure-hearted zeal to imitate. It's rather frightening to realize how much power a spiritual teacher has. I've noticed that some devout practitioners soon find that they have the same afflictions as their teachers. Not only do teachers impart the message, but also the side effects of afflictions. This is why bodywork is easy to learn, but difficult to do without also transmitting destructive energies. The therapist gets the anger and depression of the patient and the patient gets the vainglory of the healer.

However, the real harm is done to the vain person. She has deviated from the spiritual journey. It's at this stage that some high-profile spiritual teachers rationalize that they do not have time for spiritual practice since their flock needs them. They quit practicing and they do not even notice that they have no praxis. The practices of formal prayer, common life, manual labor, and *lectio divina* get forfeited because the ministry needs their undivided time. This is a risky way to live.

The true apostolic life is when the mind is still in steady praxis of ceaseless prayer, ceaseless repentance, and ascetical discipline. Apostolic life can be a way of managing one's afflictions, but only if our outreach is done contemplatively. That is, it is inspired by the Holy Spirit, done with great guard against the false self and for the praise and glory of God, done in the present moment and not with regret for the past or fear of the future. Apostolic service without a contemplative foundation can be, subtly, simply a career or project.

If I am vain, I can harm others by my example of carelessness in following ordinary disciplines and by gathering disciples who want shortcuts and instant enlightenment.

The vain person often has an overactive imagination; daydreaming takes over from the real thing. The homily is prepared, the delivery is duly given, but the fantasy continues . . . with sustained applause and follow-up invitations. Disappointment follows if the event doesn't live up to the imagination's field of dreams. There may even be resentment toward the flock that failed to appreciate the true worth of the vain person. The vain one retaliates by leaving and putting on record how defective that congregation is and how mistreated she was.

The training to prevent and treat vainglory is to give attention to one's intention as much as we do to the visible manifestation of the work. The talk, the letter, the visit, the song, the dance is only part of the thing. The inner "why" and total receptivity to God's grace guard against vainglory. God doesn't need any of us to sustain the universe. Or God does need all of us, but from our true empty self not the ego-projections of our false self.

Daydreaming, or free-fall thinking, needs to be checked. Attention, ceaseless prayer, and even no-thought can be cultivated. It's rewarding to notice daydreaming and to shift it back into unthinking. We are not our thoughts. Thoughts come and thoughts go. Unaccompanied thoughts evaporate and the still mind is at peace.

Only the seasoned practitioner who has an awareness and practice of guarding against vainglory is qualified for ministry. Manual labor is the teacher for the vain person as we learn to be attentive to our vanity and to our subtle attempts to manipulate others into thinking well of us. Just as dejection is thinking too lowly of ourselves, the affliction of vainglory is thinking too highly of ourselves. Both are forms of pride because we are focusing on ourselves and on our self-made ego. Humility is truth.

We have renounced our former way of life, but we reclaim it, using spiritual forms as our own possession, or falsely claiming others' love or honor, or doing good that others do not need done. Vanity is duplicity. It opposes the virtue that is the simple and single-minded pursuit of our heart's desire while remaining open to the truth. Our attention is split. The self-made ego grows, and God diminishes as our point of reference. We are creatures, and we create ourselves. The false self replicates the myth of the Garden of Eden in our lifetime. The tendency toward this form of independence and pride is primordial, and although it was set in motion by the generations that went before us, my own vainglory is my own personal sin.

It is dangerous to use spiritual techniques for our own self-made ego. There are those who teach altered states of consciousness through meditation practice; others who claim that drugs are an acceptable means of contemplation. This tricks both the teacher and the student into thinking drugs are somehow a spiritual benefit to the soul. Vainglory is an affliction of the soul. Drugs to lead us to contemplation are what suicide is as a way out of depression. They alleviate pain for the short term but do not contribute to our salvation. We must be willing to undergo suffering, ultimately the burden of consciousness. Vainglory works like a drug, dulling the rawness of being aware of standing naked before God.

To be a healer is more than a gift of grace that some people have and some people do not. Eastern masters talk of lifetimes between the one in need of being saved and the one who is trained to help others to be saved. Westerners jump quickly from "once lost" to now a seer and healer of others. Authentic healers using the field of body energies must undergo a series of initiations with reliable masters who have demonstrated years of training and feats of purification. And to be healed requires one to accept an invitation to become attuned and to perform the rigorous actions necessary to maintain oneself. This requires purity of thought, will, and desire; today there's a dangerous attraction to a quick fix.

Being a wounded healer can be a version of vainglory. Healed and healer requires a confirmation from another who has credentials. The spectacular, the easy, the miraculous are all traps of vainglory that require discernment to sort out whether they are from God, self, or evil.

Vanity that is skillful in doing the right things for the wrong reasons soon slips into the next affliction, which is endstage self-centeredness. The pride affliction is doing the wrong things for the wrong reason. For a study on humility, the major teachings are to be found in the many sources that address pride. There is no humility where there is vainglory. The second renunciation simply is not negotiated. Instead of renouncing one's afflictions, the vain person uses the affliction in service of the ego-self.

Pride

To stray from the spiritual journey is serious. We can dupe ourselves into thinking, we do not need awareness and wakeful receptivity. We renounce renunciation and indiscriminately reappropriate whatever comes our way. In the first renunciation, we renounced our former way of life; in the second renunciation, we renounced our inner thoughts and motivations that moved us back into our former way of life; in pride, we renounce God and become our own god.

Let's review:

- The food affliction is indiscriminate eating and drinking (gluttony).
- The sex affliction is indiscriminate use of another's body or the fantasy of another's body (lust).
- The thing affliction is indiscriminate use of things, time, talents (greed).

- The anger affliction is indiscriminate words, thoughts, and deeds that harm another (rage, hatred, murder).
- The dejection affliction is depression, or indiscriminate and undifferentiated sorrow accepted as a hopeless condition (suicide).
- The acedia affliction is a wearied soul giving up inner work ("soulicide").
- The vainglory affliction is shunning God as my innermost referent (narcissism), which requires submission, surrender, and authenticity.
- The pride affliction encourages me to authorize what good is for others. I become god for them.

There are two kinds of pride, carnal and spiritual. Carnal pride is human lack of discrimination. Carnal pride is acting on my inner conversations with thoughts such as:

Food: This food is too much and too rich, but I need to eat when I want to, only what satisfies my tastes, and as much as I need, no matter what other considerations might be. I need food to be happy and drink, too. I am very hard to live with if I do not have my usual diet, served in the manner to which I'm accustomed. If a waiter doesn't serve me promptly and with style and grace, they'll get no tip from me.

Sex: I need sex. No one should deny those natural impulses. In fact, sexual desire should be cultivated not muted. My mate is at my service. When I'm satisfied, this makes him or her happy. I also like certain outlets and entertainment to keep my sexual juices flowing. No human being should get out of practice. Sex is my favorite sport. What is life without a little fun?

Things: Things provide safety. I actually get sick if I do not have what I need when I need it. It's good for others to see the fruit of hard work and being successful. They can do what I did; no one gave it to me. I've earned everything I have. Now my possessions are almost up to my standards. I'm happier when my needs are satisfied. It's the American way and my heritage. Wars have been fought and won to give me what I deserve. The least I can do is enjoy it!

Anger: When I'm annoyed I let people know it. Nobody messes with me. I deserve the best, and when I have to wait or see mistakes I have no patience. People are incompetent. It's good for others to get a piece of my mind. Anger keeps me strong and in control.

Dejection: I have been harmed and my life is ruined. No one has suffered as much as I have. I *cannot* study, teach, or do manual labor because it depresses me to focus my mind. I just do not feel up to it. I need to take care of myself because others really do not understand what I've been through. I can dress, walk, and present my body the way I feel. No one can make me look better than I feel on the inside. That would be inauthentic. I've no reason to live and every reason to check out. There is no one who feels as bad as I do, and I do not give a damn what others think.

Acedia: I am bored and have had it with the spiritual journey. I'm beyond the ascetical practices; they no longer are any benefit to me. I've prayed enough for one lifetime. It's simply too much effort to watch my thoughts, guard my heart, remain in my cell, and be faithful to common prayer and common table. My needs are not being met. I'm ready to be the superior and be in charge. Things need to change around here. I will leave if I do not get my way.

Vainglory: I need more recognition and affirmation for all I've done. I'm the best there is and no one knows it but me. Guess I will have to leave the monastery to get the students I deserve. I'm too good for this place. The diocese can hire me. I can be a parish priest, a liturgist, a professor, an administrator, maybe even a bishop. No one is more qualified and competent than I am. If no one is going to do it for me, I will have to do it for myself. Maybe I should just start my own spirituality-training center. The disciples will flock to me.

The afflictions circle around from the seeds of pride. We can see why the tradition shortened the catechesis on the spiritual life and simply taught that the greatest sin and the root of all sin was pride:

putting oneself in the place of God. The way out of pride is to return to one's spiritual practices and to humility that replaces our "ego-selfing" with the abiding Presence.

There is still spiritual pride, and it is the final and most deadly of the afflictions. Both carnal pride and spiritual pride mean doing the wrong thing for the wrong reason. But the difference is that the reason for carnal pride is human weakness. I simply prefer eating to fasting. I feel the urges of sex, the defenses of anger and depression, and act out on my inclinations. I consent to the invitation of my inner commentary to do what I know is not virtuous. With carnal pride, there's an awareness of the law and moral rightness and that one is consciously deviating from the norm.

Spiritual pride, on the other hand, is doing the wrong thing for self-centered reasons that negate God's presence and chose the ego as the referent rather than God. The fear of the Lord that is the beginning of wisdom is supplanted by negating the existence of the Lord. The spiritually prideful person appropriates the law to himself or herself without fear. The self-righteous person lives in such a way that others fear her because of her domination and tyranny. "I (the ego-self) decide what is the good." For the spiritually proud, all virtue is destroyed and vice becomes virtue.

The first stage of spiritual pride is to renounce God as having any relevance for my life. God doesn't exist, or if God does exist, I do not care. I ignore God since it doesn't seem to make any difference anyway, or maybe there is no God, or if God does exist, God wouldn't punish me, or if God did punish me, I would not worship that kind of God anyway. I've got to find my own way. I've grown up and away from religion, which has only served to confuse and demoralize my self-esteem. I fear only not having enough time before death to get everything done I want. I know the good without God. I do not believe all that pious talk about vocation or calling. I'm called to be my own person.

The second stage of pride is the doing of evil. I receive an invitation from evil entities with power, intelligence, and an agenda in the human domain. These subtle evil bodies, often called demons, infect the proud person and offer to collude with her. Together with these superior intelligent beings, the proud one can do amazing things, actually borrowing power from another higher realm and partaking in evil.

To the proud one, however, what would have been evil in her earlier life when she was on the spiritual journey now becomes good. It's good to have disciples who worship the talent and intelligence of the teacher. I enjoy watching the deprivation of those who deserve to suffer, because they shunned me when I was their pastor or their teacher or their friend. I can offset consequences with my powers, so I do not need to be cautious in sex or in business negotiations. I will get even with anyone who gets in my way. I can transfer vibrations through my concentration. I can read hearts and know another's weaknesses and bring them to their knees. Such exhilaration! This sport is better than sex.

There is the religious practitioner with the affliction of spiritual pride who takes on devil worship and ritual sacrifice, and who in turn shares in their demonic powers. I owe these evil entities, they think, my loyalty and allegiance for the powers I have now!

While carnal pride hides in the cloak of guilt and shame, spiritual pride hides in the darkness of secrets and subtleties. No one likes to face evil or to think that there are dark forces that the scientific world *cannot* examine using empirical methods. We fear that the community or the persons involved will be at risk if we talk about it. So we keep it hushed and keep others "in the dark," feeling that talk about evil will bring on more evil. We often shun evil by denying it: "I didn't see that or hear that, or I must be wrong, or that's the stuff of science fiction, not reality." A sign of evil as an entity is that it divides and pits everyone against the other so that there is chaos and confusion. Ordinary conflict management *cannot* touch such conditions. Evil exists and it is in our midst. Evil seeds are present in ourselves and manifest themselves in carnal pride. Evil exists in manifestations of entities that have form and intelligence.

The antidote for pride is to return to the four methods of responding to any thought or feeling that rises:

1. Enter into direct dialogue with the thought and refuse the invitation, using teachings from the tradition of scripture or previous experience.

2. Replace the thought with another, either with a short affirmation prayer or with ceaseless prayer. John Cassian recommends the call to prayer (Psalm 70:1). "O God, come to my assistance. O Lord, make haste to help me" is the form we use here at Our Lady of Grace Monastery. The Jesus Prayer is the most substantive mantra that has come from the experience of the desert tradition.

3. Anticipate thoughts that become afflictions through vigilance, watching, and guarding the heart. This mode of awareness dismantles the thoughts, and soon the eye of the heart detects their first risings before they get strong enough to offer a temptation. Notice the moment of consent and get ahead of it.

4. Do selfless service with a total focus on the present moment. Being in the Presence takes all of our attention, and we experience the stillness of being.

If we use these four practices as well as manual labor, the cell, prayer, common life, and apostolic service, the afflictions will be purified. Pride will be rooted out and replaced by humility. Thinking, acting, and inner ascetical work often contribute to pride. When we unthink, undo, unwork in total surrender we receive the Spirit of Jesus. Our right effort is to refrain from consenting and going up the chain of thought. When we do that, we check our mindlessness and our ego.

Before we consider the third renunciation, there is one more teaching about the afflictions. When we pass through one of the afflictions, we can look back and see the benefit, the fruits, that emerge on the other side, purging each of the afflictions.

About Food and Drink: To observe the middle way in eating is not only healthy for the body's weight, energy, and longevity, it also is the first step in living a life of discrimination, being able to sort, to anticipate my "enough," to feel the equanimity of being satisfied, the absence of urges dominating my consciousness. When

I eat and drink mindfully, with poise and appreciation, I experience the fruits of transcending the compulsive affliction of the food/drink thought. Fasting becomes a way of life, and feasting is the way I celebrate it!

About Sex: To be continent, celibate, and chaste is to be in right relationship with my vocation. To hold the sacredness of the other and to be treasured by my community or my marriage partner, or to enjoy my state of being as a single person, is to be fully human. I am the same in the day as I am in the night. Sexual energies quicken life and all the living.

About Things: To be a gardener on this planet earth is to breathe and to work. I use things because of what I do: art, crafts, nature, reading, cooking, enjoying the entire universe. What I have for my use is enough. All is good, very good. "Things" become who I am. I am rich indeed! I take up my responsibility to preserve things for the next generation's well-being and prosperity.

About Anger: After my emotions are quieted, I have the facility to see the other's point of view and experience compassion. The forgiver and the forgiven one merge. I become an elder with bright eyes, clear skin, a quick step, and a gentle smile. Others are attracted to me, but I am at peace in my cell. Forgiveness reigns. No past diminishes my present and no future supplants it.

About Dejection: Mystery rises in place of dense fog and weighty sorrow. A smile smoothes my brow. In place of darkness, I see luminous, clear, and intense light. My spiritual senses open. My experience of depression is gone, and my thoughts become quiet. On the other side of mystery, you know that you know and are known.

About Acedia: The hard heart melts into compunction and the gift of tears cleanses me and takes me beyond returning to my former way of life. The cell becomes the home of my heart. My work is my prayer and my prayer is my work. Ceaseless repentance becomes an abiding experience of mercy. All is well. I am stilled.

About Vainglory: Glory is God's. My self actually dies. Only God satisfies. Public ministry or manual labor is equally my preference, since God is at work in me and I'm not the one doing it. Either success or failure is all right. I have a single focused energy; inner fantasies no longer influence me. All is God's way and that is my way. There is no separation.

About Pride: Humility replaces gluttony, lust, greed, anger, depression, acedia, vainglory, and self-righteousness. Purity of heart replaces fear of the Lord.

The second renunciation, or the purgative way, has purity of heart as its fruit. There is another stage, illumination, to undergo for contemplation to be abiding (*theoria*). We have seen that the first renunciation is to renounce our former way of life, and the second renunciation is to renounce afflictive thoughts that put us at risk of returning to our former way of life. In the third renunciation, we renounce our self-made thoughts of God, so that we can know God as God is and not the projections of our own ego.

3

Third Renunciation

Thoughts of God

There are many manifestations of God. Nature is replete with the creativity of divinity; the sacred scriptures are a privileged source for divine revelation; and for the Christian, Jesus Christ is the pure manifestation of God. God is all, and nothing is in existence without God. As human beings, incarnate and imaging, we encounter the existence of God through the many manifestations of this inexhaustible mystery we call God.

Christians have two thousand years of reflection and elaboration on this mystery of the manifesting God. Despite the unknowability of this ultimate transcendent mystery, we strain to know God: "faith seeks understanding." Theology, then, is the art and science of exploring and interpreting ways of knowing God and also what we know about God. There are a myriad of ways to move into an understanding of God, but here are four that will help to elucidate our knowing.

All religious traditions have attempted to name the utterly unnamable, and one approach is to reflect on the names of God: All-Powerful, All-Knowing, All-Encompassing, All-Loving, All-Merciful. There are hundreds of names for God. We study the faith traditions of humankind, even though we know that none of these names can circumscribe the reality. Rather, the names give brilliance to the unitive greatness of the divine mystery, much like the multifacetedness of diamond. Each offers an evocation of the greatness and mystery of the divine reality. Any specific name contains within itself all names, so we can enter the door of the Presence through any one of the names. We come into "knowing analogy": I know an ocean and God is like an ocean—spacious, beautiful, full and flowing, powerful, magnificent, etc.

The second approach is to list the many names of God as in the first approach but then to discard the "boat" of these names and attributes quickly and step into the light. Then we enter the chamber of light upon light. We understand that God is more than all the names, all the attributes, all the titles, and all the manifestations that we humans experience. God is indeed like the ocean, but so much more, and so we don't dwell on the initial starting point. This second approach is similar to the first approach of "all," "most," and superlative qualities attributed to God, but goes beyond it by saying that God is so much more than we can imagine, so much more than our most sublime names, attributes, or titles, that we cannot limit our affirmations to human talk. It is still an affirmation but raises the meanings to the highest mathematical power and/or cosmological plurality of forms and forces. This is moving from a to b to c . . . to the end till all is exhausted, and we merge with the One.

The third approach is to know that we "do not know," and that the intellect cannot grasp God. Yet in the Christian tradition we say that, though we cannot know God by reason and intellect, we can know God by loving. The classic "negative" (apophatic) theory from St. Gregory of Nyssa and the unknown fourteenth-century author of the *Cloud of Unknowing* states that we cannot know God, but we can love God; we beat upon the cloud of unknowing with our longing darts of love. The most that is intelligible to us is that God is and that I am. This has the effect of bringing us into not-knowing and of concentrating on loving. Where there was reason and conceptual thinking, now there is loving.

This is what you are to do: lift your heart up to the Lord, with a gentle stirring of love desiring him for his own sake and not for his gifts. Center all your attention and desire on him and let this be the sole concern of your mind and heart. What I'm describing here is the contemplative work of the spirit. It is this which gives God the great-est delight. For when you fix your love on him, forgetting all else, the saints and angels rejoice and hasten to assist you in every way.[16]

The fourth approach to God is like the third but moves further into the method of unknowing. I call it *unthinking*. We literally re-verse the chain of thinking and unthink back into the mystery of being. We come heart to heart, center to center, or essence to essence with the source of Being itself, and while we are respectful of the infinite manifestations of ultimate mystery, we refrain from think-ing about them and fall in adoration before the God Who Is.

The existence of these four approaches underscores the tentative-ness of all our attempts to know God and suggests that it may be more respectful to renounce our thinking about God, because no thought is God; it is simply our thought about God. This renuncia-tion of our thoughts of God resonates with the earliest biblical tra-dition, when Moses' attempt to wrest the divine name from God was disappointed by the divine mystery who would only say: "I AM WHO I WILL BE." From the very beginning of the revelation tradi-tions, there is an injunction: let God be God. Therefore, in this criti-cal renunciation, we do not renounce or negate God or our search for God, but we shift our effort toward humble adoration before the face of God. We renounce our self-made images of God.

An important distinction for a Christian is to recognize God when God does show up, whether this is in undifferentiated mys-tery or some kind of subtle form. We must cultivate a personal and deep devotion to this way of the Lord, or abiding Holy One, or Jesus of the gospels. It is not for us to determine the manifestation but to respond with full attention. It seems to me that we are born with a psychic imprint that knows God. The way my psyche works may differ from that of another Christian, but I know God and am known by God deep in my soul. It is according to this imprint that I can understand my path because it makes sense to me. In my own case, I have a dialogical partnership that involves a felt sense of pres-ence with Christ Jesus. For others there is an abiding in mystery that is not focused on a faith-felt Jesus. For each of us this experience of God is unique and personal. Once we know the particular way that God comes to us personally, it is important to cultivate familiarity and at-homeness, both in ourselves as creatures and in the relationship with God as our Creator.

What is important here is to let God come to us as God will, and we receive according to our original psychic imprint (the essence known before we were born). Then we consciously live our life cultivating love and devotion to the God who is planted deeply in our hearts.

What is, is. This essence-to-essence sense of God is so powerful to some mystics that they say that manifestations in the created realm, no matter how subtle, are obstacles to a truly profound experience of divinity, and so all manifestations must be negated. As the Hindus say: "Not this, not that." This orientation is also found in the Christian tradition and is known as the "apophatic" way, or the way of the negation of forms. It tends toward an undifferentiated experience of God, and some people are attracted to, or have a propensity for, an impersonal God. In the main, the Christian tradition prefers a sense of a personal God, because of its radical belief in the Incarnation of Christ Jesus, Son of God. The Incarnation is, so we do not renounce the manifestations of divinity, but we do renounce the creaturely preoccupations or thoughts about these manifestations. We simply do not think about God-in-form or manifestation, but rest in the sense of God's being. The third renunciation, then, is to shift from thinking about God to simply and humbly experiencing the God-with-us.

As a way to understand how one mystic viewed this third renunciation of self-thoughts of God, I've "interviewed" Teresa of Jesus. She taught her novices to pray using some of the most powerful methods in the Christian tradition. She fostered a spousal mysticism that recommended a form of recollection where one checks the physical senses and dwells within. You might say that she doesn't fit any of the categories I just listed above—and that's the point. She teaches that we must not have assumptions about how God is God to us. We let God be God, and use the necessary discipline to remove obstacles of unbelief and distraction, so that we can recognize God when God happens to us in our actual experience. To teach this important renunciation we will now take an imaginary ride with her to Madrid.

A Dialogue with Teresa of Jesus

Teresa of Jesus was born Teresa de Cepeda y Humada in 1515 to a wealthy family in Avila, Spain. Beautiful, charming, and outgoing, she entered the local Carmelite convent in 1536. For some twenty years she struggled with serious illness and the somewhat lax religious life of her convent. Her spiritual fervor faded, and for a year she even abandoned prayer altogether. In 1554, she experienced a "reconversion" after seeing a statue of the wounded Christ. With renewed ardor, Teresa eventually regained her spiritual equilibrium and emerged to reform her Carmelite order. In 1562, she founded St. Joseph's Convent in Avila, the first convent of the Carmelite reform. A tireless worker, she founded sixteen more convents before her death in 1582 at the age of sixty-seven. Teresa's extraordinary insight into the process of spiritual growth has been transmitted through her writings. *The Life* is an autobiographical work that tells of her own spiritual development up to the point when she founded her first convent. Works that present her spiritual teachings are *The Way of Perfection*, written for the sisters of St. Joseph's Convent, and *The Interior Castle*, her most thorough and methodical description of the spiritual life.[17]

Meg: Can I ride with you to Madrid? I'd love to talk.

Teresa: Yes, do come along. It is a day's ride from here. We can talk, but sometimes I will ask for us to observe silence.

Meg: Fine. Shared silence with Teresa of Jesus sounds like heaven to me!

Teresa: What's on your mind? Is this interview about prayer? You can only talk so much about prayer without profaning the experience. That is why very soon books, lectures, and conferences do not help. Reading and talking is thinking. Doing little things with extraordinary love is better than books and talking to enter into deeper realms of prayer.

Meg: I thought you said books are helpful.

Teresa: Books help at first. I insisted that my novices be literate. After some years most of us feel no inclination to read during prayer times. Yet a major obstacle to prayer is ignorance, so reading at other times can help. But it is not helpful to read just anything. Reading helps us to know ourselves. Reading can give us self-knowledge based on what others know. Self-inquiry is necessary for beginners. It also helps to have a competent spiritual director, though skillful directors and confessors are woefully rare.

Meg: I know from your story you had many ill-advised confessors who caused you confusion and grief.

Teresa: Yes, it is so difficult to trust your innermost soul to another mortal. I tried time and time again to find a competent confessor. I was disappointed many times. Some priests even made a sport of "testing" me and my resolve. Most distressing! But I learned obedience.

Meg: How do you know if you can trust a spiritual director? It seems to me that if he or she disagrees with me, I feel that he doesn't understand; and if he agrees with me, he might be as deluded as I am.

Teresa: This is discernment. You place your trust in Our Lord, and then you ask Him to send a mortal that can help you discern His will. Directors need to be pious and virtuous. However, when you are more advanced it is necessary to find someone who is learned, too. But, as I say, most of the time I found that Our Lord gave me clear counsel directly to my heart. Conscience is the highest law, you know.

Meg: Can you trust that all your inner thoughts are of God?

Teresa: I do not trust that all my thoughts are of God, but I do trust God. He'll let me know His wishes and He knows my heart. I tell my novices to stay in constant prayer and share everything with God. I shared all my frustrations with His Majesty.

Meg: You speak of His Majesty. Did he come to you as a king? Was he always dressed like a king?

Teresa: I had no expectations of how, when, and where His Majesty would come to me. Most of the time He didn't come at all. You know for eighteen years I had utter dryness and had only traces of fervor. But when He did come, it was always in some form that I could recognize. I'd be gazing at the crucifix or a statue or simply the altar, and the encounter would swiftly draw me in. My heart knew Him and He knew me!

Meg: So, when you teach your sisters, do you have them imagine Our Lord in their thoughts, like with the woman at the well, or walking along the road to Emmaus?

Teresa: No, to meditate I taught them how to rein in their senses— their ears, eyes, smells—and to bring their mind to their spouse. Most of the time we let our mind wander in all directions. This free-fall wandering cultivates distractions not respectful attentiveness. I taught my nuns to bring their senses into their hearts and rest there in faith: God's presence is in the castle of their soul.

Meg: Is this your famous practice of recollection?

Teresa: Yes, without recollection there is little capacity to receive God's visitations.

Meg: Is the practice of recollection the reason for enclosure?

Teresa: Enclosure is the cell of your heart. We go to a monastery that organizes this solitude, just as the desert fathers and mothers did long ago. We close the doors of the senses. We live in solitude. This readiness yearns for intimacy with the Divine. Prayer is just another word for waiting upon the Lord.

Meg: Did you ever think you were imagining Our Lord and that Our Lord wasn't really there, but that you were into a self-made fantasy?

Teresa: Oh, Meg! I could never have contrived such powerful surges of love between us! Those revelations were singular graces. They came unbidden. I suppose my imagination can dupe me, but these visitations were way beyond a mortal's invention.

Meg: I thought you said that these revelations came when you were in recollection?

Teresa: No, recollection was my ongoing practice that disciplined my mind and helped me know myself, but Our Lord came only when He wanted to.

Meg: So, why did you need a spiritual director if Our Lord came to you directly?

Teresa: I needed help to understand what was happening to me. For forty-three years of my life I lived above the river surface, as you would say. Then, Our Lord wanted this intense relationship. I wanted to be sure that I was honoring Our Lord's visitations by doing His bidding. I had such an intense desire to do nothing that would displease Him.

Meg: The confessors gave you a hard time from what you wrote in your story.

Teresa: They could not understand me. If you have not had this experience, you *cannot* connect. You do not learn this in books! I felt I was often misjudged as being either a hysterical woman or a demon-infested maniac. You *cannot* imagine how much suffering it caused to be so discounted and subjected to such acrimonious scrutiny. This was so intimate and personal. They'd ask the rudest questions!

Meg: Do you think you received singular and extraordinary revelations that are rare? So, how could anyone understand you?

Teresa: Yes, those revelations were given to me, an unlikely soul. As you know I was worldly, tepid, and attached to social convention until I was about forty-three years old, but don't let me retell my story here.

Meg: Am I to understand that most of us won't have those revelations? Most of us will not have actual appearances of Our Lord? Will we have to wait till our next life?

Teresa: You can have intimacy with Our Lord now in this life without dramatic revelations. Most of us can come to Our Lord through ordinary ways of praying or living. It's not up to us to determine how God comes. God comes as God wills!

Meg: Do we invite Our Lord, or can we invite the Holy Spirit or the mystery of the Holy One or even Mary? I had a Jesuit spiritual director who taught me how to meditate. We'd set up the scene and use our imaginations. You know that practice. I notice that you didn't teach that to your novices.

Teresa: You are right. I didn't feel that applied meditations contrived by someone else ever matched my own experience, so I taught my novices to ready their hearts and minds, and then let God come in whatever form He chooses.

Meg: This is an important distinction. Tell me again what you are doing when you do recollection.

Teresa: You open the invitation to receive God, but then God comes as God wills. We renounce our self-made concepts of God, and let God be God. For me Our Lord came as His Majesty like a king, a ruler, a spouse inviting me to a spiritual marriage. For others, you would have to ask them, but it seems as though it's more abstract, like the enveloping mystery of Being.

Meg: Please go on. Do you mean to you say that all of us can be contemplatives and experience a felt mysticism?

Teresa: Yes, why not? The carriage has stopped. The drivers must be watering the horses. Let's get out and walk. We need to stretch our legs.

Meg: Yes, you were just about to tell me how we could all be contemplatives.

Teresa: God is the Holy One. We are creatures made in His image and likeness. We feel an attraction for God that *cannot* be denied. Our desires surge beneath the surface, ready to erupt at the slightest encouragement from our will. We can let distractions invade our thoughts with this and that, but in moments of loneliness, or aloneness, we know that we know there's something more that wants to be at the center of our attention. We really do not wander far without feeling the magnetic attraction to come back home to the center of our hearts. In silence we feel this longing, so we go to a place of solitude to enter this castle, as I call it. You might name it the realm of the soul, just as I live in the realm of Spain under the rule of His Majesty King Philip II.

Meg: Go on. Then what?

Teresa: It's all God's grace, this attraction and our response, but we must open the door of our hearts from the inside. Our Lord is not an intruder. We must individually accept Our Lord's offer to dwell within us, as a felt presence. However, each of us must initiate the invitation for Our Lord to come to us.

Meg: And how do we open this door?

Teresa: We close the senses to other in-breaking images, feelings, invitations, and conversations. This closing the doors of our sight, hearing, tasting, feeling, smelling is called recollection. We rein in our senses and bring our mind's eye to our attention. In faith—and this is the important aspect of intention—all this is "in faith." We are not negating the objects of our senses because they are evil or wrong; what we are doing is bringing our attention to God in faith. We neither affirm nor negate. John of the Cross and I had conversations about how to describe our prayer and contemplation. I think we both followed the desire of our heart. I have used many allegories to describe the spiritual journey but always came back to the question: Who are we to "name" the experience of God? We humbly expect God to show up, since having faith is to act as if God is present rather than to act as if He is not present.

Meg: So, then . . . in recollection you experience God?

Teresa: In recollection we detach ourselves from our senses. We let go, or let be, and accept what is. We face our fears, attachments, illusions, ambitions, and hostilities. We return to the center of our hearts and find love and remain there in faith. Our senses are like wild horses at first, wanting attention, nurturing, and acceptance. At first we feel lost and even fearful. Then we are stilled. Soon, and very soon, in that quiet we rest.

Meg: Is this the prayer of quiet?

Teresa: Yes, that's what I call it, and eventually the active recollection becomes the passive prayer of union. But let me caution you to hold all these terms lightly. Just as God comes as God wills, and we have no control over the many manifestations of God, we *must not* get hung up about prayer stages, phases, and theories. They are just hints to describe the quiet. Do you know what I am talking about?

Meg: Yes. I find my senses get stilled when my body is stilled. So first, I sit, stand, or lie relaxed and still.

Teresa: In stillness you realize how wild the mind has become. This is why prayer demands formal times: times that have a starting point, a middle, and an end, periods that have a fixed duration, for instance, an hour. The body seems to require a time of stillness to enter into this prayer of quiet.

Meg: But as nuns we pray a lot in church. Isn't that enough?

Teresa: No, it is not about quantity. During my first twenty years in the convent, we gathered for prayer five hours a day. I thought that my observance was enough. Deep down, though, I knew I was distracted, and that I was using my prayer in common to avoid personal prayer in my cell. My soul was tepid, and my mind wandered in church as well as when I was not in church. I squandered my vocation. I was attached to casual social visits. I neglected my Spouse. I was not living my vows.

Meg: So, what made you change?

Teresa: Our Lord confronted me. I felt such true sorrow. I was wasting my time and going through the motions of being a nun.

Meg: When you realized your wrong direction and had a change of heart, what did you do? Did you return to your cell and offer your vows again as you did as a novice?

Teresa: Yes, I did rededicate my vows to My Lord, but I found in my cell I was just as distracted as I was in church. This dryness was difficult. I began to practice recollection and bring my senses into the cell of my heart. His Majesty blessed me with great consolations.

Meg: Tell me more. You needed time alone, and in that solitude you needed a practice to stay in the cell of your heart and in the cell of your monastic living quarters.

Teresa: Soon, and indeed very soon, I found that my monastic cell was more like an apartment with my own kitchen, staff, and guests staying months at a time. Or sometimes I'd go visiting some relative or friend and stay with them for months at a time. It was obvious that I needed to start over someplace with only people who would help me to get back to the original spirit of a cell.

Meg: The cell in the monastery is just a room, is it?

Teresa: Yes, the cell is a place to practice discipline of the mind. Without such practice the body might be in the cell, but the mind is back in the parlor talking to Countess Constance.

Meg: Tell me, then, about that practice of the mind in the cell.

Teresa: You welcome Our Lord to come. On your part you bring your senses within yourself. Grace happens. Stillness follows.

Meg: Would you say that for prayer of quiet to happen you have to renounce your senses and your body's liberty to move at will?

Teresa: Yes. And you also renounce deciding how you receive Our Lord's coming . . . sometimes as a brother, a friend, a helper, or lover. Our Lord sometimes doesn't come at all. Silence might be the presence.

Meg: But you always feel His presence?

Teresa: No, sometimes no felt presence, but felt faith.

Meg: What do you mean by felt faith?

Teresa: I know that I know. I have no sweet presence of a lover or friend, but my faith is strong.

Meg: Have you ever lost faith?

Teresa: Yes, this is a dark night. I had months and even years when I had no felt faith, and had no memory of presence.

Meg: What did you do?

Teresa: Suffered.

Meg: How did you stay faithful?

● *Teresa:* I stayed faithful by not running away. I resisted the temptation toward despair that would discount my desires. I was determined to be faithful, I longed for intimacy, and I wanted to be awake and found waiting when Our Lord would return.

Meg: Do you think that your desire merited you the gift of union?

Teresa: No, I merited nothing. My being was finally pared down to its nothingness, and when all the dross had melted away, I discovered the union that was there all the time. In nothingness I experienced union.

⌈ *Meg:* Did you have presence of yourself? I mean, where was your mind during all the years of suffering?

Teresa: That's the best question you've asked me. . . . Yes, I had presence, or, as you'd say, "consciousness" of myself, and I'd bring that awareness to prayer and lift that up to His Majesty. I never lost a keen sense of interior awareness. I didn't know what to call it, but in this sense I never lost God's presence because I was aware, keenly aware.

Meg: So internal awareness is God?

⌊ *Teresa:* Yes, it's the breathing and knowing that you are breathing.

Meg: Doesn't God have another form besides ordinary life?

Teresa: There's nothing ordinary about life! We've gone in through the side door of mystery. Creatures *cannot* define God; we can only receive God as God.

Meg: If ordinary life is where God is, why did you reform the Carmelites? Do you need such an austere monastic life to find God?

Teresa: It's not for finding God that we need contemplative structures and practices. It's to find ourselves. We are distracted, not mindful, unaware, and so dissipated. I reformed my order because we had returned to worldly ways.

Meg: You had such an urgency to make those seventeen new foundations so that those who'd live there would stay put and get serious about a contemplative life. Would you say that contemplatives in the world could also enjoy a mystical life?

Teresa: Of course. It depends on one's vocation, or calling, and then being faithful to the Teacher within who guides and nurtures you.

Simply put, we are all contemplatives in the heart, and we have to honor that place in the heart. How to protect this inner core depends on one's responsibilities and commitments. I find that everyone can practice recollection to some degree, but I think it is more difficult in the so-called world. There are so many distractions! But as I can testify I was in the monastery for thirty years before I made a choice for contemplative living. I made a choice to change my structures. I think everyone can do that at some point in his or her lives. For example, when the children grow up and move out, the parents can choose more solitude.

Let's sit here by the stream for midday prayer, and let's eat our lunch in silence so we can hear the sound of this little stream. Those birds are rare, and can be seen only in these parts.

Back in the carriage the conversation continues.

Meg: What about Jesus? Does Jesus come only to select Christians? I've heard some say that God is Mystery, and that the humanity of Jesus is too gender-defined for their taste.

Teresa: Some of my nuns used to say that to me, too, that Jesus was part of their childhood but no longer part of their piety. That's not my experience. Our Lord has no human limits, but we do. He comes in humility so we can grasp Him. He became the human Jesus for us. The Holy Spirit will blow at will, and I know there are other ways to the Mystery, but Jesus is here for us.

And, let me go on here, as this is important: I, too, had a director who told me to move "beyond" Jesus. I tried and found his advice harmful on two counts: One was who was I to define how the experience of God is to manifest itself to me? And secondly, I'm an incarnate being, so why would I object to a human manifestation of God?

Meg: You sound so orthodox. Why did you get in trouble with the Inquisition?

Teresa: We *cannot* fathom the graciousness of God. I think there was an attraction to mysticism that defied the categories of Scholasticism. I couldn't prove my revelations . . . and they couldn't prove they didn't occur! There was also such a fear of the devil at the time. In fairness to the vigilance of the church authorities, there were plenty of pseudo-mystics around absorbing attention and notoriety. The authorities felt compelled to protect the faithful who looked to them for authentic guidance.

Meg: It seems from your writings that you had a great desire to be a daughter of the church.

Teresa: Yes, it's important to be obedient and always to suspect your own self-serving motivations. Humility is to be willing to surrender and let God be God in your life.

Meg: So, you surrender your life to God. And you also surrender your need to make God fit your ideas of God? Can the church help us with this?

Teresa: Today you might say that the church is a means for discernment. The church is complex and has many voices. One must learn to sort out the voices of the church.

Meg: So, sometimes the church is wrong?

Teresa: The church is a human instrument! I chose to reform monastic life within the church rather than separate out. I have difficulty understanding why some chose to go a different way, since the unity of Christ's body ought to be visible on earth as well as in heaven. However, working with existing church and civil structures was my greatest challenge.

Meg: I have another topic I need to ask you about. Do you think penance and austerities are means for holiness?

Teresa: In my earlier years I did mortifications to curb my willfulness. Later I realized that I had to renounce penance, because it was just another form of selfishness and even pride. My body was always prone to illness, and to follow the demands of being a reformer was enough penance. I really didn't have to invent ways of suffering to demonstrate my resolve.

Meg: So, is doing penance a temptation or an invitation of grace?

Teresa: Life's ordinary vicissitudes are enough penance, and life itself is the ordinary means of grace. Novices should be taught recollection and to read and memorize scripture and the early elders. Novices need to be attentive to their thoughts in silence and to watch their motivations and curb idle talk. They need to be taught how relationships either bring you closer to God or distract you from your heart's desire.

Seems like we are stopping again to rest and water the horses. Enough talk for now.

Later, riding along in the carriage over barren landscape.

Teresa: Let me ask you a question, Meg.

Meg: Certainly.

Teresa: Why are you going to Madrid?

Meg: I'm not, really. I just wanted a time to visit you. The nuns said you were going to Madrid. I would have gone anywhere you were going to have this privileged conversation.

Teresa: Company along the journey is indeed a privilege. That is why I refounded the Carmelites to be small intimate communities. We can do it better in groups of souls who are like-minded. Life is difficult and has so many twists and turns.

Meg: So, do you consider your way of life living alone together?

Teresa: No, I consider us living with Our Lord together. We form a little community of believers who share things and support each other. I do not see the strength to be actual hermits in our times. Too much aloneness can be selfish and self-serving. Few have the strength to be hermits. Doing it together is safer and more profitable. You need enough solitude to reach stillness and to develop your own intimate relationship with your Beloved.

Meg: Finding a loving community is more difficult than finding a spiritual director.

Teresa: Who said it was always loving! I founded monastic communities for the sake of contemplation. Conflict is not all bad. We can use our difficulties to test our resolve. Community life is difficult, but that is our desert. We are Carmelites following the desert elders of one thousand years ago.

Meg: When living together in common, each of us needs solitude, silence, and stillness. You do not have to be a nun to practice recollection and become centered and aware.

So, do you advocate training in practice or merely waiting upon the Lord's initiative?

Teresa: Yes. Our Lord can suddenly surprise the devout, but a contemplative practice keeps you present and ready to hear that still, small voice inviting you. The support of a like-minded community in this effort is invaluable.

Meg: For Christians is Our Lord always our Beloved, or is awareness of an impersonal God a higher form of God's love for us?

Teresa: Remember our earlier conversation about renouncing how Our Lord comes. For me, a gradual deepening into the intimacy of a Spouse was the way I described our evolving relationship. But God comes as God wills. For Father John of the Cross it seems to be more about Being in Mystery, rather than a personal relationship as it is with me. So, each of us renounces our self-made thoughts of God, as God comes as God wills. God made each of us, and God knows that our hearts are made for Him.

Meg: I guess if we renounce our self-made thoughts what we get in exchange is Truth.

Teresa: The truth is that all speculation must be renounced. Thoughts about God are not God, it seems to me. But make sure you also do not renounce your *relationship* with God. I tell my nuns to let God come as God wills, but you come as you are. Tell Him everything, the details of your life, your longings, hopes, dreams, and frustrations.

Meg: Then aren't you making in your mind a human image of Jesus and creating your own manifestation?

Teresa: Important point. I learned this distinction from Jesuits who lecture these days. Applied meditations and scriptural *lectio* have their place, so does the liturgy, but in our personal prayer we cultivate our own presence before the Presence of God. When we bring our own presence, we bring our human details. We bring ourselves as we are and reign in our senses that dampen our awareness. Then we can see God.

Let's take some silent time now, so that we can rest our wild imaginations and close the door on our senses.

Almost at Madrid . . .

Teresa: Meg, are you awake?

Meg: Yes, I was noticing the fields covered with wildflowers. I do not remember them when I passed through here just two days ago.

Teresa: What was on your mind when you came through here then?

Meg: I was preparing for our visit. I wanted to get my questions together and was practicing in my head my interview with you.

Teresa: What were you doing with your mind when we took our rest from talking?

Meg: I practiced recollection. I drew in my sight, sounds, emotional reactions, thinking apparatus, imaginary conversations, and sat still, at least as still as I could in this bouncing carriage.

Teresa: Did you remember God and fall quiet?

Meg: Yes, first I remembered myself, where I was and why I'm here, and my desire to be like you someday. Then I remembered God. It was better than a nap. Restful.

Teresa: One of the fruits of contemplation is that the ordinary senses meet the inner core of stillness, and this deep rest from constant alertness rests the nerves. When we are not focused "out there," the spiritual senses open. The other fruit is that you get to know yourself.

Meg: Spiritual senses. What are spiritual senses? How do they differ from ordinary senses? Do I have spiritual senses or are they a special gift, like your revelations?

Teresa: That would take longer than the time left before we part company in Madrid, but let me invite you to more and more recollection and prayer of quiet. When you return to your senses, you see that nothing is ordinary anymore. The smell of flowers, the redness of red, the sound of a brook, the touch of a friend, the feel of the morning air, the weight of a rock—all have a freshness and energy that quickens. A degree of gratitude and grace opens from deep inside. All matter is alive and engaging in this wonderful time we call living. Spiritual senses see what was always there, but hidden from view, because the ordinary senses were concealing the revelation.

Meg: So, my spiritual senses see what is really there, whereas my ordinary senses see only outer manifestations. So, what seems is not the whole of it. When the spiritual senses open, we can trust that the way it "seems" is the "way it is."

Teresa: Yes, children often see "the way it is," but their senses get dulled over time. Through contemplation we return to our senses!

Meg: You teach us to close off our attention from the natural senses. Do the spiritual senses open in their place?

Teresa: That might be too simple. We need our natural senses for everyday living. We withdraw our attention from our natural senses to expand our awareness into mystery and being. This awareness springs up as Presence. In the Presence we learn new ways of seeing by faith. There's a whole mystical dimension that has to be experienced rather than speculated about. The mystical experience is "more than" our natural senses can grasp.

Meg: Are the spiritual senses the human way to see God?

Teresa: Rather, it is knowing that you are seen. Here we are at our destination. Our conversation has made the journey go faster!

Meg: Thank you for this precious opportunity. May I call on you again for another colloquy?

Teresa: Shared silence is sweeter!

The Illuminative Way

Teresa of Jesus gives us ways of thinking about prayer and stages of the spiritual journey. The third renunciation is even more important today with our growing awareness of Eastern religions and of pluralism within faith traditions. St. Teresa is an example of humility that comes with being faithful to the way God comes to one. She also integrated the inner praxis and outer practice of the monastic way of life. Her practice of recollection is portable and can be used by anyone, anytime, anywhere.

When God as God shows up, the person is in the light. If this experience is ongoing, we describe the person as being in the illuminative way or living with the fruit of the third renunciation. Another example of an illumined master is St. John of the Cross—he was Teresa's contemporary and friend, a poet and a philosopher. His teachings on the spiritual life are not speculative theory, but a systematic reflection on his own experience. I find him, like his elder sister-friend Teresa, to be an example of this third renunciation. It is easy, though, to misinterpret his meaning, if we, who are mostly in the second renunciation of the purgative way, project that stage into his teaching about the illuminative way.

Briefly, I'll tell you what I mean about the danger of misreading him. I find that he speaks about greed, lust, and gluttony, but he is not talking about the greed, lust, and gluttony encountered in the second renunciation to those who have tasted the inner light and had the felt experience of mystery. The greed, lust, and gluttony of the third renunciation involve stepping sideways after having tasted spiritual delights. The person becomes insatiable for felt experience in the mystical realm.

The dark night of the senses is about the spiritual senses being shut out of the actual felt Presence. The dark night of faith or of the soul pertains to having not only no consolation of the spiritual senses but also no memory "in faith" of those consolations. Both the felt Presence and felt faith in the Presence is dark or negated. The pain is suffering beyond suffering as a heart that was fully satiated by the Presence is not only empty and void of satisfaction, but there are often struggles and afflictions of the mind, and the Evil One could also be at work in the soul.

I do not know much about the dark night of the senses or of the soul either personally or from the people who have come to me for spiritual direction. Dark nights are a stage on the spiritual journey after enlightened experiences. Most of the time when I read about dark nights or hear about them from others, I hear about afflictions from the second renunciation rather than from the third renunciation, which is renouncing self-made thoughts of God. It seems to me that the proficient practitioner has enough experience of light to claim that he or she is undergoing a dark night of the soul.

In any event, what matters for the practitioner is not to know what stage she or he has reached, but to take refuge in Jesus Christ who knows exactly what it entails for humans to renounce their concepts of God and to stay vulnerable so that God can move us from light to light. The light that emerges on the far side of the afflictions of the third renunciation is what Gregory of Nyssa calls "dazzling darkness." Self-reflexiveness is inappropriate. Questions such as "How am I doing?" "What stage am I at?" are meaningless here. The illumined self is flat on her face in adoration.

The illumined person renounces not only concepts of God but also any thoughts about the experience of God. It seems that those who have experienced "the light" *cannot* share the story. Such sharing could never be part of a spiritual autobiography, let alone an entrance essay for some program or novitiate. No one who has experienced this dazzling darkness would ever attempt to tell you about it. Indeed, Our Lord cautioned the three apostles after his Transfiguration to tell this experience to no one.[18]

So, in the third renunciation we know that we know. The silence and experience of *theoria* (contemplation) is the destination of the journey. There is profound transformation in the stillness of the realization "that God is and that I am."[19]

The journey continues: We are to renounce our self-made thoughts of self.

4

Fourth Renunciation

Thoughts of Self

To renounce thoughts of self is the fourth renunciation. With the presence of God burning in my heart, I no longer need to be involved in conversation with myself but direct all my affections toward the felt presence. So the renunciation of the thoughts of self really becomes renunciation of self-talk. This happens in two ways. First, there is no self to talk to or from. This means that one's interior chatter is free of that self-made self. Second, there is such a felt presence either in experience or in faith that to talk to the self is regressive. The true self longs for the Other. The Presence is so abiding that there is always a Thou in the mind's eye and ear. The "I" is caught up in relationship. This is the zone of the fourth renunciation.

In this abiding Presence we stand before the Mystery empty of our previous ways of knowing and being known, respectful and conscious about what comes from the inner center of our being. God as God rises in consciousness. For the Christian this manifestation from our inner senses is understood as Father, Son, and Holy Spirit. The church gives us ways of interpreting this presence. Theology and dogma sharpen our intellect with distinctions. Precise language helps us to remain close to the teachings of Jesus.

This fourth renunciation is to renounce the self-made thoughts of self. I am not qualified to write about this but do know it to be true. Furthermore, I personally do not know anyone who abides in this fourth renunciation, but we have an embodiment in Thérèse of

Lisieux. As a child who lost her mother when she was four years old, she had a self-centered personality. At age fourteen she had a conversion experience that shifted her from "selfing" to sacrifice. From this saint we see that humility and all the teachings about humility *cannot* be part of one's daily bread until there is a grace to shift from "selfing" to sacrifice.[20] Humility seems to be grace and not grit. If one puts on the teachings about humility before one has the grace of that shift from "selfing" to sacrifice, one risks being sick, sadistic, and self-deprecating instead of self-renouncing. The "egoic" mind has millions of tricks that lead one to alienation from the true self.

Since I am out of my depth even to write about this, I would like to shift to the literary technique of an interview with Thérèse, so she can be our teacher.

A Dialogue with Thérèse of Lisieux

Thérèse of the Holy Child Jesus was born Marie Françoise Thérèse Martin in 1873 in Alençon, France, into an intensely devout family, which nurtured her profound spiritual awareness. Thérèse's mother died when she was four years old, and for the next eight years she struggled with an overly sensitive and timid personality. On Christmas Day, 1886, before her thirteenth birthday, she was released from intense suffering and received the gift of "love and a spirit of self-forgetfulness." Thereafter she prepared to become a Carmelite and obtained hard-won permission to enter the Lisieux Carmel at the age of fifteen. Rejecting the extreme penances common at this time, Thérèse practiced unspectacular self-denial, recognizing that everyday events have spiritual value. Her final illness and death in 1897 at the age of twenty-four was marked by physical suffering and excruciating spiritual darkness, which she endured for souls without faith. She wrote fifty-four poems. Her autobiography, *The Story of a Soul,* is a compilation of three manuscripts written from 1873 to 1897 (Manuscript A, 1873–1895; Manuscript B, 1896; Manuscript C,

1896–1897). In it she describes her Little Way of recognizing our nothingness and offering the depths of our poverty to God, expecting everything from God and trusting in His merciful love.[21]

Meg: Can we talk?

Thérèse: I would love to. I promised to do more from heaven than I did while I was on earth.

Meg: In your autobiography and in the testimonials of your sisters for canonization, we get the picture that you were a troubled child. Your mother died when you were four years old. You were bereft when your older sisters entered Carmel. Was your protracted illness a mental affliction? You even worried that you were under the influence of the devil. This is not idle curiosity on my part. How did you go from such self-centeredness to self-donation?

Thérèse: Good question. I know where you are coming from. You want to know if saints need to have a prior grace that shifts the self from the center of one's ego before it makes any sense to be humble. This is an important teaching that fits my practice of the Little Way. Let me walk you through this simply, but carefully.

Meg: Thank you for understanding my question. We probably need to describe the night of your conversion, so our readers will know what we are talking about. Do you want me to describe it, or will you?

Thérèse: Thanks for your willingness to tell the story. It's probably better if I retell the experience. This will give me another chance to say it in the words of your contemporaries: I was thirteen years old, and after Midnight Mass on Christmas of 1886 as I was going upstairs to take off my hat from church, I overheard my dear, weary father saying, "Well, at least this is the last year we need to fill the child's shoes with gifts" (as was the custom in France at the time, like Santa Claus now). It pierced me to the heart. I was profoundly changed. My sister saw I had tears in my eyes and begged me not to go downstairs and just cry like a child. Since my mother died nine years previously, I had been a spoiled child needing special attention. I was so sensitive and chronically depressed. Suddenly, my heart was filled with compunction. I realized that I was a child no more. The depression that had gripped me during my childhood for the past nine years was over, irrevocably over. I was an adult and self-possessed, in my own skin. It was a sudden grace that enabled me to give of myself with enormous love and zeal, rather than to be always demanding others to love me. I had been insatiable in my demands for affection, attention, and affirmation. Now I was insatiable to sacrifice myself.[22]

Meg: It seems as if there was no intermediate phase. You were self-centered and with that grace of Christmas 1886 you received well-being and simultaneous other-centered zeal.

Thérèse: Yes, as you would say, I shifted from "selfing" to sacrifice without a middle phase of self-satisfaction and equanimity. My well-being shifted into needing to help others in place of my former way of life. I had needed so much affirmation, attention, and special care. But that Christmas Eve I grew up and knew it. My neediness was transformed into a great big heart needing to be for others. I was stunned into tears, but these tears were not wounded pride. I was weeping with gratitude.

Meg: Let me continue the story. I want to see if I got this right . . . this amazing grace. Very soon after this conversion you also shifted into a mystical way of loving. You had this felt grace of self-donation. You experienced Christ's redemptive love for us and placed all that grown-up love at the foot of the crucified one. You vowed not to let one drop of his blood touch the ground but to catch it and return it with your own love. What does that mean in our contemporary language?

Thérèse: I had this felt love. I returned it to Our Lord thanking him for His sacrifice that redeemed us so irrevocably. This is not so much to be understood as to be experienced, but let me again make it clear that all my love got united with Our Lord's sacrifice. We were in this wondrous love together. My wounds were no longer separated from His wounds. I actually had a real part to play in this love that could transform, save, and sanctify others. I could really sacrifice like a priest who ritually celebrates the Mass. My suffering had meaning, purpose, direction, significance, and even consecration. I knew that my suffering could actually substitute for and replace the suffering of others. When I was a child, I caused others to suffer: my saintly father, mother, sisters, teachers, and relatives. I was so spoiled!

Meg: Slow down—let me get this. Your love was accepted and returned and taken again along with our savior's love on behalf of others?

Thérèse: Again, this is experience. Not speculation. Words fail. I appreciate that you see the immediate shift of grace. As a child I was in need of instant return for my frail efforts and also of continuous affirmation of my little acts. I was obsessed with being good, but it was to magically accomplish my will. This grace of Christmas 1886 brought no return but only that of self-surrender to Our Lord on behalf of all, just like his suffering. We did this redemptive suffering together. The language is symbolic as there's nothing that can adequately translate this into human terms, but you understand what I mean.

Meg: But why must the suffering continue, if He died once for all and saved all of us? Why doesn't He save us from suffering?

Thérèse: Suffering with Christ on the cross is the Christian way of transforming our selves and the whole cosmos. It's not about time, as we know it, but an event in which we participate through our historical lives. Redemption has already happened but is not yet experienced in time.

Meg: I understand that you had this sudden grace both to understand the meaning of suffering and the cross and to place your very own self in the wounds of Jesus, as you say in mystical language. Can we all do this?

Thérèse: Your real question is to ask if grace, sudden or gradual, is needed to make the shift from self to sacrifice.

Meg: Yes, that's my question. Without this conversion from self to sacrifice, humility could be a version of sick self-loathing that is so prevalent today.

Thérèse: Childish love is absorbing, requiring adults to nurture and bring enough support to the ego so the child feels cherished and treasured. But there can be this shift just like the tide that goes in and in and in, and then making a reversal, goes out and out and out till at its lowest ebb it is no more. My grace was that it was no sacrifice for me to become other-centered since I had no inclination or desire to return to the limits of the ego. I can even own the language of annihilation. I, Thérèse, was nowhere to be found, in one sense, and in another sense I found myself ready for a major work of emotional donation. You wrote earlier in this book about stilling the mind of thoughts by keeping vigil. I learned to still my emotions by watching them and replacing them with sacrificial love.

Meg: Slow down once again. Let me get this. You agreed to the need of a grace either sudden or gradual to make the shift. You also said that the ego-self was annihilated, so that there was no striving after this conversion. So, what was there to donate emotionally?

Thérèse: Now, you are asking about the practice of the Little Way. Emotionally, after my conversion, I had a radical urge to give, but I was just as vulnerable as before my total conversion of Christmas 1886. I even had a heightened sensitivity to the insensitivity of others. I was so, so awake that a glance, a word, a gesture of disdain caused immense suffering. Before my conversion I suffered. After my conversion (the grace given to grow up), I still suffered, but until then I had suffered without loving suffering. Whereas from that day I felt a deep, true love for it.

Meg: What could be suffering inside you since you had given your ego-self away?

Thérèse: This is a paradox, is it not? My suffering before and after my conversion was that of being human, of being in relationship with others, being in love, out of love, and being misunderstood, ridiculed, ignored, manipulated, or used. I think there might be a mistaken notion that to have zeal diminishes human love and emotions. This was not my experience. My love got fierce, strong, intense, and dense with feelings, raw and real. I had a huge capacity to love and be loved. My emotions were like oceans poured in and out from one universe to another. The grace was also commensurate.

Meg: So your suffering was . . .

Thérèse: Being human, very human. My suffering was the raw experience of this human condition.

Meg: Maybe I'd understand better if you'd put in contemporary language two other significant events of your life. Can you tell me again about the wedding invitation that you wrote for your vow ceremony in 1890 and also about the Act of Oblation that you and your sister Celine made in 1895?[23]

Thérèse: My invitation for my vow ceremony might seem childish and romantic to an untrained eye, but it's as real today as when I wrote it a hundred years ago.

Meg: If you were to write it today what would you say?

Thérèse: To all who want to witness to the love stirring within and without, you are invited to a reception in honor of Thérèse and the human Jesus, the Lord Christ of heaven and earth. The actual marriage happened from all eternity, but now come and celebrate the bride and the bridegroom who will shower love on you as much as you have the capacity to receive. We are one, this Lover and the woman I call myself. Join us. You will never be the same after this celebration.

Meg: Does this have anything to do with sex, gender, or the social contract of a civil marriage?

Thérèse: No. Is the moon the sun? You and I both know married men and women who have this kind of mystical union with Our Lord.

Meg: Can anyone do this today?

Thérèse: Those who know of this experience know that they know. For you, it was your thirtieth birthday, right?

Meg: Yes, I was giving a homily, and it came from a new center, and I made a promise to be for others rather than for myself.

Thérèse: The shift was irrevocable, right?

Meg: Yes, but I didn't make any oblations. If you were to make an oblation today, what would you say?

Thérèse: I was seventeen years old that June 9, 1895, when I had that awakening to be a victim, not as an object of wrath, but as one who accepted suffering so others didn't have to. Suffering not only had meaning but was a means for others to come to eternal salvation. I wanted to formally accept that vocation. So, with the permission of my superior and along with my sister Celine, we made a ritualized oblation before the altar.[24]

Here's what we said in contemporary language:

Lord, we bow our whole being before you. You loved us first and we are gathered in your radiant presence. This life is precious, with your life joined with ours from the inside. In thanks and gratitude, we accept this blissful gift and return it to you with our whole body, mind, and soul and offer our very beings to you for you to use as you wish. We see that you can take us with you in this work of redemption and use our earthly lives as fuel to burn for the salvation of others. This mysterious holocaust is our deepest desire, and we come in the tradition of all the ritual and actual sacrifices offered from time immemorial. Please accept this oblation.

We understand that all suffering is to be gladly received and wholeheartedly returned, purified of any self-gain. You and you alone accept our offering, and we give our love totally and without reservation. We have nothing to give except love and to accept your merciful love in return. Justice and heroic adventure are not required, as we understand that you want to give me merciful love. As you receive this offering, we also ask for a confirming sign that you accept this. Amen.

Meg: Did you get a confirming sign?

Thérèse: Yes, a few days later I was in church and I felt a burning sensation. I thought I was going to die. I tried to get others to make this oblation, but it seemed too radical. I never looked back and actually didn't need anyone else to confirm how real this was for me.

Meg: Didn't it hurt to be a victim all the time?

Thérèse: Another paradox: I loved so much that being a victim-soul was the only satisfying way for me to express my zeal. You do not feel hurt when you serve the one you love. It feels quite natural and I found my stride doing ordinary things with extraordinary love. Nothing was too little or too much.

Meg: So you practiced the Little Way?[25]

Thérèse: Yes, It all came together for me . . . my vocation as merciful love, offering my emotional way of life as my holocaust, being little and loving directly through ordinary life.

Meg: How does that work in actual living?

Thérèse: I offer to Our Lord the small sacrifices that came to me in the routine of community life. I took up as my apostolate that of smiling at another when it was the last thing I felt like doing. I took all the little occasions for my practice. The Little Way finds joy in being pleased to be the person who you are, whoever you are. It is a way of coming to terms with life not as it might be but as it is.[26]

Meg: So, do we need to have all of these things—a Christmas Eve grace, a mystical marriage, an oblation as a victim for substitutive suffering, and a confirming sign—to practice the Little Way?

Thérèse: No. You asked me about *my* life and this is *my* story. The gift for others is that I come with the Little Way. In God's amazing generosity, I can intercede for others from this realm to your earthly life. Practice the Little Way and you will have this life of total self-renunciation. There are no requirements like having to be a Carmelite nun, doing heroics of ascetical discipline, having a mystical marriage, and making an oblation of substitutive suffering.

Meg: So, what is the Little Way?

Thérèse: The Little Way is a moment-by-moment habit of offering ourselves to merciful love. We need not be a perfect soul; it is sufficient to present ourselves to God as we are. The depths of His mercy are attracted to the depths of our poverty. Instead of relying on our own spiritual accomplishments, we must rely only on the strength of His arm. This is an ordinary way. God will reward littleness if we bear with ourselves in spite of our imperfections. This is a short, quick, straight way. All you need is to have the desire of union with God. *"Whoever is little, let them come to Me."*

I like the image of being in the arms of Jesus. He lifts me up like an express elevator. The smaller you are the easier it is to be lifted up. In the paradox of littleness, we become lighter and not weighted down by anxiety, guilt, dread, and heaviness. Littleness cuts the bond that drags us down. We practice expecting everything from God. We practice letting go of anxiety, fear, and self-centeredness and rely on God. We have nothing. God is all. So we own, accept, and face our nothingness. The "little" part of the Little Way is all about nothingness. The "way" part of the Little Way is about renouncing attachment to any emotions or feelings. Even when desires are dried up, we feel our desire for God. This ache is just part of the littleness.

Meg: So, isn't this making being sad a way of life?

Thérèse: No—there is no feeling sorry for ourselves. In faith we offer our emotional life to God. We renounce sadness. So, the "way" in the Little Way was all about renouncing dejection and using these very emotions as prayer for others. One good thing is that there is no disdain of creatures. My experience of nothingness is a method of restraint from any illusions, false expectations, or return on emotional investment.

Meg: So there is no program of asceticism added to ordinary living. You said you slept for seven years at morning prayers. In those days didn't you have to do a penance for that?

Thérèse: Carmelite monastic life was harsh in the late 1800s. I just didn't do it—those personal programs of flagellation, hairshirts, and mortifications. I just offered my ordinary life, and my superiors blessed the Little Way.

Meg: We find that zeal can often be a form of pride. Did you learn this from studying St. John of the Cross?

Thérèse: I admired the brilliance of St. John of the Cross. He renounced all "thought" of God in prayer. In my doctrine of the Little Way, we have a renunciation of "affect" in the whole of life. Thoughts come and go, and if you shift your thinking to something else, the thoughts do not keep their hold on the mind. But feelings linger, last, and fester. The Little Way is to surrender all those feelings, moods, ups and downs that come from hurts outside and memories rising from the inside. This emotional asceticism is the Little Way. Also, we never take a vacation from giving all. There are no days off from this practice as emotions rise every day and everywhere.

Meg: Is not renouncing your emotions a form of repression?

Thérèse: Another good question. Thanks for the clarification. I suppose I should say I renounce commentary and attachment regarding my emotions. It means full consciousness. We face and receive our emotions, such as anger, depression, and the drag of the human condition. We face the self-made illusions about ourselves. Therefore, to renounce our self-made thoughts about emotions is to embrace truth. There is no ego-self to nurture. The Little Way is to literally prefer nothing to Christ.

Meg: There's nothing childlike about this, as it is a mature full-bodied love. The Little Way seems like a practice of Cassian's fourth renunciation: the thoughts of the self.

Thérèse: God calls all to holiness. The Little Way is without ecstasies or spiritual revelations. We have great desire like Joan of Arc but do not have miracles or outstanding works. Hiddenness, like that of the Holy Family Jesus was born into, sets a pattern for us. Our role is to be found, loved, and fashioned. God always loves me first. I am a child to be carried. I present myself empty of all preconceptions of holiness. To live by love is to navigate endlessly, sowing peace and joy in every heart. The Little Way substitutes for vows of consecration, oblation, and any other form of asceticism. Those are rituals that sum up the practice, but the practice itself is enough for anyone to do and to be faithful in giving all. I had an image in my heart that no drop of blood that flowed from Jesus on the cross would be spilt on the ground, but would be caught by my little acts of offering. This is mystical language, but I know you understand beyond words that there is a doing it together . . . this redemptive love that prevents others from suffering and making restitution for all the sins ever committed.

Meg: I'm not sure I am ready for this teaching on mystical substitution, but I do get the significance of practicing the Little Way. You are saying that, if we accept the invitation to follow your invitation to practice the Little Way, that is the same as your grace of Christmas of 1886 to shift from self to sacrifice.

Thérèse: Yes, and the Little Way is the ordinary way. You do not have to be a Carmelite nun who is ritually married to the Lord. You do not have to make an oblation to a superior. The Little Way is simply the practice of using your life as a prayer. And the Little Way is to have the little, ordinary affective moments of life offered with big faith in God's merciful love.

Meg: Being little I can do this! I offer my very littleness as my prayer and it becomes redemptive suffering for others. Amazing!

Thérèse: You know that a definition of prayer is to offer your thoughts to God. The Little Way is to offer your emotions to God.

Meg: So the Little Way is the contemporary form of humility?

Thérèse: Yes, humility is the experience of being human. You simply offer that back to God.

Meg: Sounds so easy. Why is it so hard?

Thérèse: When it seems hard, remember you are not alone. I'm spending my whole heaven doing good on earth! I'm an emotional heartbeat away.

The fourth renunciation is to renounce thoughts of the self. A warning needs to be sounded here, lest confusion overtake the profundity of this teaching. We do not renounce or negate the self, as this would be death dealing. We renounce the thoughts, commentary, judgments, and chains of emotional programs that accompany the

false self. The true self is mystically in union with Christ Jesus, who
is one with the Trinity. This is mystery, for sure, but intelligible
through faith.

On the far side of each of these four renunciations is humility,
the face of humility.

5

Humility

A Dialogue with John Cassian

We are ready now for the teachings on humility from the desert tradition. They make sense in the light of our four renunciations:

- to renounce our former way of life and take up a life following the words and deeds of Jesus
- to renounce our thoughts and intentions that are not toward God
- to renounce our self-made thoughts of God
- to renounce our ego-sourced thoughts of self and shift from self to sacrifice

The language and worldview of our desert elders sound harsh to our contemporary ears. Their directives toward renunciation seem negative, life denying, and emotionally immature. However, humility matters so we need to retrieve these teachings and reclaim what is appropriate for our times, no matter how difficult the task. The reward is amazing because thoughts matter: behind or ahead of the thoughts is Presence.

In this last chapter I would like to interview John Cassian and let him speak for himself. There are many teachers of humility, but in John Cassian's *Institutes* he makes a case for humility being the way of life of a Christian that replaces the way of life under the yoke of the afflictions so painful in one's former way of life. In this dialogue he is the teacher and I will be the disciple. I have a companion, Sister Bridget, for this imaginary interview. This is the same method Cassian used in his *Conferences:* to ask questions of the teaching elder. Sometimes the questioner was Cassian's traveling companion, another monk, Germanus. To avoid repeating teachings that have already presented in previous parts of the book, in this fifth chapter I will have Cassian referring to those sections "as if" he actually has already read this book. Here is a short profile of John Cassian's life.

John Cassian seems to have been born in Dacia (now known as Romania) about the year 360 C.E. He left his native land while in his twenties or thirties and, with his friend Germanus, joined a monastery in Bethlehem. From there, still with Germanus, he twice visited Egypt in order to acquaint himself with the riches of Egyptian monasticism. It was from Egypt that the two friends set out for Constantinople. After ordination to the deaconate by John Chrysostom, he went to Rome and was ordained to the priesthood by Pope Innocent and eventually made his way to Marseilles. He died in the early 430s.[27]

For the purposes of this interview I will ask him to teach me his ten indicators of humility as he has described them in *Institute* 38.[28] Remember that these institutes are a compilation of John Cassian's interviews of desert fathers in Egypt and Palestine in the fourth to fifth century C.E.

Meg: It is an honor to be in your presence. Sister Bridget and I have come a long way to find you. I understand that you are starting your own monastery here in France based on what you have learned in your travels in Egypt and Palestine.

Cassian: Yes, we are establishing two monasteries here in Marseilles, one for men and one for women. How long are you going to stay with us?

Meg: We will be here only two days. We promised to be back in our own monastery for the final profession of Sister Gertrude. We were wondering if you would teach us about humility. Do you have time to have a conference with us?

Cassian: Two days to learn about humility! We might have enough time go through the ten indicators of humility that I teach our novices here.[29] We can begin today between supper and compline and then we can finish tomorrow before you leave. Come to the front gate after supper and I will take you to my study near the library.

Meg: Certainly. We will follow you. I have not even heard of the ten signs of humility.

A short walk to a circular room between the library and the refectory.

Cassian: Yes, make yourself comfortable. I will sit here behind my writing table. Few visiting monks know these ten indicators of humility. I am happy to share them with you.

He lowers his head and reads:

The beginning of our salvation and the preserving of it is the fear of the Lord. For by this the rudiments of conversion, the purgation of vice, and the preserving of virtue are acquired by those who are being schooled for the way of perfection. When this has penetrated a person's mind it begets contempt for all things and brings forth the forgetfulness of one's family and a horror of the world itself. By this contempt, however, and by being deprived of all one's possessions, humility is acquired.[30]

Pausing . . .

Cassian continues . . . Humility, in turn, is verified by the following indications: First, if a person has put to death in himself all his desires . . .

Cassian stops reading, looks out the window. That opening paragraph will make sense at the end, so can we start with the **first indicator: to put to death all desires.**

Meg: This language is exactly what closes books, shuts ears, and brings a yawn to contemporary readers. Do you mean this literally? Certainly not!

Cassian: "Putting to death desires" must be accepted as fact. Let me explain.

"Desires" is plural. Remember these teachings on humility are for contemplative seekers. One desire is necessary. Other desires are not negated but renounced for the sake of the one desire: for God.

Meg: Then why not say that our main desire is God and that we can move in a God direction? Do all the other desires have to die? This death to desires sounds ungrateful to my ears.

Cassian: There has to be the willingness to deny oneself, pick up one's cross, and follow Christ. This is strong language and a persuasive motivation to move through the renunciations. This first indicator of humility is for one who seeks God. The language is direct but doable. The grace is to embrace the cross of being single-minded. This ultimate concern has the effect of keeping you toward God.

Meg: I thought desires came from God, too. If I put to death all my desires, wouldn't I be dead? I feel like my truest being, what I call myself, is "desire." My life juice is to have desires. Feelings and full-blown passions are what it means to be human. Isn't it good to be human?

Cassian: Slow down. Yes, to be human is good, even very good. And to have desires is also good. The first sign of humility means to be able to lay aside my desires for the sake of the one desire: that for God. You might accept more easily the fact that God is your heart's desire and you have the discretion to refrain from any obstacle impeding progress toward your deepest desire.

Meg: So then, would it be okay to teach your first sign using the language of affirmation rather than negation?

Cassian: Like what? How would you say it?

Meg: To have one desire: God.

Cassian stroking his beard . . . That is the idea, but the humility part of the truth is that you are willing to deny yourself anything that is not consistent with your desire for God. Renunciation is your part of the relationship necessary to receive God as God.

Meg: Why is that? Can't I affirm all my desires and collect them into a God consciousness? Isn't that humble, too?

Cassian: Notice your language. You are collecting and you are affirming. God is God and you are to stand naked-in-being before God, since you are not God. God emerges in splendor and light, warmth and transcendence, when we are receptive. God is all. We are to renounce anything and everything that is not toward God.

Meg: So to put to death my desires is to let God be God? Is that possible? Is this a language problem here or something I am resisting?

Cassian: Probably both, so let me try again to explain what I mean:

1. Self-made desires pervade ego consciousness and one forgets God.
2. Then we notice our thoughts, and notice our attachments to thoughts.
3. Then we need to renounce our attachment to these self-made thought constructs.
4. When these attachments die and thoughts get stilled,
5. God springs up.
6. Or I could say that the presence of those desires is replaced with the presence of God.

Meg: So, let me get this straight. Is it the "multiplicity" of my desires that is not God or is it the "content" of my desires that obscure God?

Cassian: Both. The simple truth of God emerges when we renounce our self-made desires and get next to our soul's image of God, who is One.

Meg: I'm going to need to ponder this.

Cassian: The second indicator will shed light on clearing the obstacles that block our desire for God.

Bridget: What is the second sign of humility?

Cassian: **The second sign of humility is that you conceal from your wise elder none of your deeds but also none of your thoughts.**

Meg: My students would want to know why anyone would care about their thoughts or deeds. Who reveals what to whom? And how would that help me with my heart's desire? And do you manifest everything that you think about and everything you do? Who has time for that?

Cassian: Remember these teachings are for those on the spiritual journey and those who feel inclined to the contemplative life. Given the invisibility of the spiritual journey under the river, as you call it, there is plenty of opportunity for self-deception. Humility thrives in the light, unlike deception, which festers in darkness. As to your question of "who" reveals "what," let me respond:

The seeker comes to a wise elder, who is skilled in overcoming the afflictions. The seeker reveals thoughts to the elder that have entered her heart.

Meg: This discipline and training is about the eight afflictions?

Cassian: You might not have all eight afflictions. One affliction can teach us purity of heart. Even if you have only one affliction, you can confess your thoughts and dismantle its patterns. It is not "talking about" our afflictions that is required here, but, rather, an elder listens with the ear of the heart, which is a technical term for receiving another with the spiritual senses open. The disciple lays out thoughts as they come to awareness. In the light the chain of thoughts is broken and the grip of intensity is moderated. The thinker observes the thought. There is poise between the thought and the consent, the intention and the action.

Meg: What sort of thoughts do I lay out?

Cassian: Your heart's desire is God, right? You lay out the thoughts that prevent you from prayer. We are called to remember God.

Instead we think of ourselves, our hurts, our burdens. Speak your heart as you do when you pray or even the way you are talking to me right now.

Meg: Tell me, what good would that do? Is that not just rehearsing my woes?

Cassian: No, since you are not your thoughts, when you speak them aloud to another they trail off like a vapor. Thoughts and attachment to thoughts lose their grip when you give voice to what is rising in your heart. This manifesting of thoughts is a way to experience the release of thoughts that cycle round and round and move from ideas to action, from incidental behaviors to full-blown patterns of habit. Handing them over frees you of their tyranny.

Meg: I certainly know the plague of obsessing on my inner thoughts. My mind can get in such tangles. Does saying your thoughts out loud really help?

Cassian: Yes, the practice helps you see your thoughts in the light. After a while you can get ready for the chain of thoughts and know their patterns. Then these thoughts will not surprise you, nor can they build up and magnify into compulsions.

Meg: To whom do I speak my thoughts? We don't have elders and teachers as you did in your day.

Cassian: Elders are around; you just don't know them. In the meantime, you and Bridget can do this for each other.

Meg: Bridget, do you see any advantage in doing this? If we did this for each other, we would need to know more about the method.

Bridget: Father John, does the one who receives the thoughts reflect and give advice?

Cassian: No admonition is necessary. The mere confession releases the cycle of thoughts you speak of in chapter two on the eight afflictions.

Meg: Again, tell me what relationship does this practice of manifesting of thoughts have to humility?

Cassian: As with all experiences, you'll know when you do it. To share in words your inner thoughts without commentary, without putting yourself up or down, and without any embellishment provides the climate for truth and honesty with oneself, others, and God. Soon you will see how all this fits together. We can continue with the third indicator of humility.

Bridget: Yes, if there are ten signs of humility we will need to get through at least five of these signs this evening.

Cassian: **The third is to do nothing by your own discretion but to do everything according to the elder's judgment and to listen eagerly and willingly to that elder's admonitions.**

Meg: This sounds like the monastic vow of obedience. This is a tough saying today even to monastics, and how can contemplatives living in the world make sense of this third sign of humility? How can anyone today be tied to another's will and wishes? Isn't this fostering codependence?

Cassian: No, this is not regressive. This accountability is maturity in its eloquence. It is difficult to explain, though. Let me try. Your heart's desire is God. You get to know yourself when you are attentive to your inner life: urges, impulses, thoughts, choices, motivations, actions, patterns, moods, and passions. You also know that by yourself you are weak, inconsistent, and need help. There is a natural desire to seek guidance and to be directed by someone to whom you can entrust your soul because you share a thirst for God. To be able to ask another to listen actively and give support and advice is a gift. You are saying in truth that you do not know everything and that you need to be accountable, so you can be steady in your resolve for this spiritual journey below the river and to not return to your former way of life above the river.

Meg: I meet with Abbess Margaret once a month, but I never thought of it as part of being humble. I have a list when I see her.

Cassian: And . . . what do you discuss or ask?

Meg: I compile a monthly list in five categories: Do you want to hear my list?

Cassian: Briefly!

Meg: First, there are routine items I simply report: what happened during my last absence from the monastery,

Second, I ask permission for new things, expenditures, time commitments, or projects.

Third, there are some items on our agenda, like taking more persons on in spiritual direction, I not only want permission to do but I also want a blessing.

Fourth, for big things, like writing this book, we take most of my conference time on the questions I'm discerning.

Fifth, once in awhile, I will ask her to make the call and "tell" me what to do.

Bridget: The last time she told you what to do, you didn't like doing it!

Meg: But I did it anyway, didn't I? Also, I want to add that Abbess Margaret brings her agenda to our conversation. I look forward to these conferences. She gives me quality time, and I also come prepared and take time afterwards to make notes and reflect.

Cassian: What you are exploring in those conferences is what takes place above the surface of the river. That is obedience, but there's a deeper level of practice that would strengthen your vocation. If you got into the practice of manifesting thoughts and seeing your motivations, your attractions as well as your afflictions, you'd see the benefit of being in a relationship of obedience, which implies accountability. This is a deeper degree of humility. You manifest your thoughts and you submit to move toward your promised vocation. You actually submit to the authority of another for the sake of following your calling, which is your single-hearted desire for God.

Meg: This vocation seems to be the calling for humility. Tell me again the relationship between vocation and humility.

Cassian: Prayers are those acts by which we offer or vow something to God. This is called a vow in Greek. For there is a play on words. In the Latin one of the psalms reads: "I will pay my vows to the Lord." The dual meaning of the word means that it can also be expressed as: "I will make my prayers to the Lord." And what we usually read in Ecclesiastes: "If you vow a vow to God, do not delay to pay it," is written similarly in the Greek: "If you make a prayer to the Lord, do not delay to pay it." The word for *vow* means both pray and pay.[31]

Meg: I don't see the connection between prayer and renunciation.

Cassian: This will be fulfilled by each of us in this way.

> We pray when we renounce this world and pledge that, dead to every earthly deed and to an earthly way of life, we will serve the Lord with utter earnestness of heart. We pray when we promise that, disdaining worldly honor and spurning earthly riches, we will cling to the Lord in complete contrition of heart and poverty of spirit. We *pray* when we promise that we will always keep the most pure chastity of body and unwavering patience, and when we *vow* that we will utterly eliminate from our heart the roots of death-dealing anger and sadness. When we have been weakened by sloth and are returning to our former vices and are not doing these things, we shall bear guilt for our prayers and vows and it will be said of us: "It is better not to vow than to vow and not to pay."

According to the Greek this can be said: "It is better for you not to pray than to pray and not to pay."[32]

Meg: I'm getting the picture. My moral life is also my prayer life.

Cassian: Work and prayer is the same thing. I pray as I work and work as I pray.

Meg: I get this now. This is about the one working and praying, not the work done or the prayers said!

Cassian: The moral life is a prayer. Without a moral life there is no prayer, except to ask for mercy. **Let's take sign number four and you'll see how this all fits together. In every respect the disciple maintains a gracious obedience and steadfast patience.** This specifies that the quality of obedience is freely given and the patience is steadfast through good times and bad. Humility has indicators of graciousness and long-term patience.

Meg: This makes sense for contemplatives on the spiritual journey, since we have given the whole of our life, all of our life, to answer God's call.

Bridget: I can see that someone in the affliction of acedia is neither gracious nor patient!

Cassian: The indicator of humility here is to remain positive and continue freely accepting relationships as gifts along the way. If the two of you would manifest thoughts to each other, and if you continue to will and refuse the same things, no afflictions would get in the way of either your friendship or your desire for God.

Meg: I am beginning to see the softer side to the teachings on humility. What is the fifth sign?

Cassian: **The fifth sign is to neither bring injury on anyone else nor be saddened or sorrowful if anyone else inflicts harm on you.**

Meg: So much for the softer side! Is this real? Isn't it a sign of health to be aware of harm done and not be in denial?

Cassian: I'm glad you're asking these questions so candidly. The fifth sign of humility is neither to harm another nor to be saddened or sorrowful if harmed. It is easy to see why to harm another is a violation of humility because who are we to allow ourselves to do so? If the challenge of this teaching addresses the way we fall into dejection when we are harmed, the benefit is that we know that with God's grace we can accept pain and not become depressed.

Meg: This sounds impossible to me. I've known depression that came from harm. Isn't it the natural effect of being hurt? Harm hurts.

Cassian: A culture of depression is endstage captivity. Remember the teaching:

Elders differentiated between moments of temptation. There is the *prosbōle* (suggestion in thought), which is free from blame (*anaitios*). Next follows the *syndiasmos* (coupling), an inner dialogue with the suggestion (temptation), then *palē* or struggle against it, which may end with victory or with consent (*synkatathesis*), actual sin. When repeated, such acts produce a *pathos* (passion) properly speaking, and in the end, a terrible *aichmalōsia*, a "captivity of the soul," which is no longer able to shake off the yoke of the Evil One.[33]

Meg: It's beginning to make sense why noticing our thoughts is so important.

Cassian: Yes, remember the teaching goes on to say: The proper object of *exagoreusis tōn logismōn* (revelation of thoughts) is the first stage of this process, the *prosbolē*. One must crush the serpent's head as soon as it appears.

Bridget: This part I remember: All this is done through an entire strategy: *nepsis* (vigilance), watchfulness, the guarding of the heart (*custodia cordis*) and of the mind, prayer, especially the invocation of the name of Jesus, and so forth.

Cassian: So, we now understand the theory about the thoughts. Now, return to our practical example.

Meg: We were talking about harm done to us.

Cassian: Yes, in humility we can accept harm done to us as a natural consequence of being alive and well. Who of us can escape the human condition? I know that there are causes of depression that are not in the realm of consent, but a sign of a humble person is one who endures hardships with sustained patience and refrains from retaliation.

Bridget: This is a most countercultural sign of humility. I feel that it is weakness to passively accept harm. Where's the justice?

Cassian: Justice is eclipsed by peace. The goal of purity of heart and selfless love means that our justice is different from that of the world. Forgiveness, going the extra mile, loving one's enemies, becomes the content of our justice, rather than setting the record straight, getting even, and making others pay for their crimes. When peace pervades the heart, there is no enemy, no one is deserving of judgment. God is the judge. We are all in need of God's mercy.

Meg: These signs of humility are getting harder to do, but not more difficult to understand. Can we do number six before we retire for the night?

Cassian: Yes, sign number six would be a good stopping place for our discussion. **The sixth sign of humility is to do nothing and presume nothing that neither the general rule nor the example of our forbearers encourages.**

Bridget: So a humble person has to mute any originality?

Cassian: No, that's not the intent of this sign. This presumes that the humble person feels the solidarity of being in relationship with others. This indicator is a willingness to learn from those who have gone before us and to learn it from the inside, not from the outside as an observer.

Meg: How can contemplatives not living in a monastery be humble since they do not share in the common life?

Cassian: Everyone, even hermits, live in relationship. This sign of humility is to search out those contemplatives who either lived before us or are living now and to be in stride with them. What I cannot stress enough is that humility is not knowledge or a theory or a scientific speculation, but is a direct way of living from the inside. Humility can only be known through experience. The common life is only one way. There are others. The sting of humility is to do what others have done, learn from tradition, and refrain from thinking that I am so special that no one has invented a contemplative way of life for the likes of me.

Meg: Does humility have to sting?

Cassian: I'm not sure. No one has asked that before. Let me ponder that.

Bridget: This still seems vague to me. I can see the monastic way of life, living in common, but what does one do if one does not live in a monastery?

Cassian: Let's go back to vocation. This is a calling to a particular way of life. So if you are married or monastic or single, there are others who have gone before you and you live the life as a married, monastic, or single person. We do not choose the type of vocation we are called to. Each of us is called, and in that calling there is a way to live our heart's desire.

Meg: So, if married I'm married, if monastic I'm monastic, and I live that form of life in the tradition of those elders who were seeking God. But what if there are no elders in our time that we can follow?

Cassian: Then you follow the elders in the tradition. There are always re-starts. That's what this book is about, is it not?

Meg: I hope so.

Cassian: Yes, now it's late. To be refreshed we must rest. It is time for compline. Return here to my writing table after morning vigils and we will go through the remaining four signs. Sleep well. And remember to observe silence. In the stillness of the night, silence is the teacher!

Meg: My thanks for your time this evening. This is more wisdom than I can possibly remember. Bridget, we'll need to take time and recall what we've heard today. Thank you, Father John.

Bridget: We will see you here tomorrow after vigils. My thanks, too.

The next morning.

Cassian: Did you rest well?

Meg: Yes, but not without a sober dream about getting lost on a dusty road and asking several other travelers where we were going. Nobody seemed to know.

Cassian: Your fears are sorting out some frustration, but with God's grace all will be fulfilled more satisfactorily than any dream can imagine. Let us continue with our teachings. Are we on the seventh sign? Bridget, are you ready to continue? I see that you seem to be the one taking notes.

Bridget: Yes, I took time to put together my notes from last evening. I do have some questions, but they can wait till we have looked at the other four signs of humility.

Cassian: Good! Let us continue. **The seventh sign is being satisfied with utter simplicity and, being an unfit laborer, considering herself unworthy of everything that is offered.**

Meg: I hear your words, but I'm not sure what this sign points to. I do not feel unworthy. I feel grateful, but not unworthy.

Bridget: Meg, did it ever occur to you that you might not have all the ten signs of humility?

Meg: Thanks! I get the humor, but I resist this sign. Why must we feel unworthy?

Cassian: I wish I could dilute the word or say it doesn't mean what it indicates or that it's just "sort of" feeling unworthy. My experience is that I do feel unworthy. I am an unlikely soul to be given so much from God. I would be honored and satisfied with much less than I have. Does this make any sense to you?

Bridget: Can I try to interpret it for Meg?

Cassian: Certainly.

Bridget: Meg you have such a great devotion to the Annunciation of the Angel Gabriel to Mary and also the Visitation of Mary to Elizabeth. In both of these events the women proclaim the "who am I" question that sounds to me like they feel unworthy of the honors bestowed.

Meg: Now, when you use those examples, I can identify the times that I've been so surprised, and I guess, "unworthy." Do you remember on the way here how that boat came back to the dock and got us because we were late for the departure? They were so glad to do it, too!

Cassian: So, you get the seventh sign, which is to feel the littleness that St. Thérèse spoke about in your interview as her Little Way. Shall we proceed to number eighth? We still have three more teachings.

Meg: Yes, these indicators of humility are beginning to make me cringe. Humility is a lifetime effort! What is the eighth sign?

Cassian: **The eighth sign builds on the seventh: One does not declare with one's lips alone that she is inferior to everyone else but actually believes it in the depths of one's heart.**

Meg: I can't detect any difference between sign seven and sign eight.

Cassian: Sign seven is to claim being unworthy of grace. Sign eight is to own this status deep in your innermost heart. We have some time here. Let me see how far I can go into this teaching. Actually feeling the experience God's mercy is an example of being on the far side of afflictions.

Meg: Is anyone on the other side of the afflictions of food, sex, things, anger, dejection, acedia, vainglory, and pride?

Cassian: Yes, the afflictions come and go, then cycle around again in ever-new presentations. But if you are on the far side of even one of the afflictions, you could enter into this eighth sign of humility. You feel compunction. This unique grace is to be pierced to the heart and convicted of your need for God's mercy. There's no way to describe it from the outside, but if you had felt it from the inside, you would know of what I speak. Once this has happened, there's no return to self-righteousness. Your innermost heart is stabilized in the cross of felt mercy.

Bridget: I have seen this happen to others, it has not happened to me yet, but . . . I've seen others. My mother had this. . . . Tears, lots of mellow tears that never seem to dry up.

Cassian: You'll know when it happens. The heart needs no more convincing that God's love holds your very being in existence. Authentic compunction seems to be returning today. Many who pass through this monastery have experienced compunction.

Meg: Since they could hardly brag about this singular grace, how would you know?

Cassian: Hearts do not need conversation. In silence there is a knowing beyond speech. Shall we continue?

Meg: Yes, of course.

Cassian: **The ninth sign of humility is this: One holds one's tongue and is not loudmouthed.**

Meg: So you understand others through silence? And the disciple shares through silence. Why would refraining from speech be better than talking? Again, we were taught to use our verbal skills and keep improving our communication patterns. We are to assert ourselves and know how to contribute to conversations. Dialogue is talking, isn't it?

Bridget: Let me clarify for my notes. The ninth sign of humility is that of someone who holds her tongue and also someone who refrains from talking loudly?

Cassian: Remember these are signs of humility. Silence is an interior practice that we do in solitude. Silence is to still the thoughts and to watch thoughts come and go. If one is vigilant in silence, one can see that most thoughts that rise need no accompanying words or actions. They come, they go. If you simply watch them, they go sooner without any hesitation. Eventually we get skilled in noticing thoughts that are actually inspirations from the Holy Spirit. These thoughts we accompany with our desire and continue cultivating in our efforts toward God. So, we are coming full circle. And, by the way, dialogue is mostly listening, isn't it?

Meg: Yes, dialogue is speaking from the heart. In the silence of my heart I know my thoughts and I can make choices to consent to the ones that are from God and, if acted upon, take me to God. Conversely, I hold my tongue to move into this inner work of the practice of silence, so that I can make conscious choices, namely, refrain from those actions that take me away from God.

Bridget: A loud mouth. Is that code for mindless speech?

Cassian: Again, remember these are signs. I cannot emphasize too strongly that the indicator of humility is revealed in speech. The tongue reveals the heart. Words, and especially many words, trick the mind to shift into the ego-self and away from the sacrifice that you teach in the fourth renunciation.

Meg: So, a sign of humility is silence?

Cassian: Yes, humility is respectful silence that is accompanied by full presence in the body's decorum and poise. The way one sits, stands, walks, and bows all speak with more eloquence than words.

Bridget: Is that the tenth sign: our body?

Cassian: You are close, but **the tenth sign is about laughter. The humble one is not ready and quick to laugh.**

Meg: Is humor against humility?

Cassian: This laughter is what tradition names ridicule, sarcasm, or derision. A humble person would not make sport of another. It's harmful to make someone the object of mirth by putting them down and making them of no account.

Bridget: This makes sense. If I felt God's loving mercy, I'd never want to embarrass another.

Cassian: Laughter is part of our well-being. This sign is to avoid being quick to discount another and place yourself outside the circle of compassion.

Meg: Are these signs listed in the order of seriousness? Is it a bigger sign that there's no humility when there is harmful laughter than when there is no accountability to an elder?

Cassian: I would rather put it this way. Laughter that harms another would not happen if the other nine signs were present. Conversely, if one thinks that she or he is humble and laughs at another's ill fate, then that person needs to start at zero again. Humility is living from the inside, being loving and sharing the human condition along the journey of life. No one should be an object of my superior wit. Humility is the experience of solidarity in the human condition.

Meg: I understand. Are there more signs than these ten?

Cassian: Yes, but these are enough.

Bridget: I do have a few questions from our session yesterday. May I ask them now?

Cassian: Yes, one or two questions would be helpful. I want to make sure we are seeing the whole of this teaching. Whenever there are steps, degrees, signs, moments, phases, and other teaching devices, I fear losing the whole meaning while we factor in the parts.

Bridget: Humility is not a virtue or the opposite of a vice from what I gather. Is it a practice?

Cassian: No, humility is not a practice either, since we would not know where to start or what constitutes humility in any given situation. Some use the word *fruit*, as humility is the outcome of the practice. Others call it a *disposition* or *attitude*. I find all these words, *fruit, disposition, practice, attitude*, have their limitations.

Bridget: So then, what is humility?

Cassian: I like your description in the beginning of this book, where
   you call humility "the face of purity of heart." It is what someone else would see of your purity of heart. You know it when
   you see it. You also know when it seems absent. I prefer to call
   humility the way of being in the image and likeness of Jesus. You
   said you had another question?

Bridget: I think you've answered my other questions. To be Christ-
   like as we see Jesus described in the gospels is humility.

Meg: You said you would return to that opening summary statement
   that was so difficult to hear.

Cassian: You mean this quote?

> The beginning of our salvation and the preserving of it is the fear of
> the Lord. For by this the rudiments of conversion, the purgation of
> vice, and the preserving of virtue are acquired by those who are being
> schooled for the way of perfection. When this has penetrated a per-
> son's mind it begets contempt for all things and brings forth the for-
> getfulness of one's family and a horror of the world itself. By this
> contempt, however, and by being deprived of all one's possessions,
> humility is acquired.

Meg: Yes, even after our conversations about the ten signs of humility, this summary seems daunting. Can you open that passage a
   little more?

Cassian: Why don't you try to explain that teaching now that you
   know the ten signs?

Meg: At the end of that same chapter 4 of the *Institutes* you have
   another version of that summary:

> According to the Scriptures, "the beginning" of our salvation and "of
> wisdom is fear of the Lord." From fear of the Lord is born a salutary
> compunction. From compunction of heart there proceeds renuncia-
> tion—that is, the being deprived of and the contempt of all posses-
> sions. From this deprivation humility is begotten. From humility is
> generated the dying of desire. When desire has died all the vices are

uprooted and wither away. Once the vices have been expelled the virtues bear fruit and grow. When virtue abounds purity of heart is acquired. With purity of heart the perfection of apostolic love is possessed.[34]

Cassian: And in your own words that means?

Bridget: Let me try. I've taken some notes here. Fear is fully dissolved into love when compunction pierces the heart. After this grace—the shift from self to sacrifice—there is a zeal that endures all for the sake of the heart's desire. While the afflictions still cause suffering, purity of heart thrives instead of the former way of life. The face of this purity of heart is humility. With single-hearted zeal we join Christ's suffering for . . . I think I'm missing something.

Cassian: You certainly grasp the teaching and almost sound as if this comes from experience, too! You didn't get to the part of the teaching that explains how our humility transmutes suffering into redeeming love for the healing of the world, but you certainly already have the idea.

Meg: One last request: Will you please bless us?

Cassian: Certainly, May God bless and protect you on your journey.

Grace

Poem by Ann Deignan

I lay one night
by an open window
in early summer
when the fragrance of magnolia
leaves behind the velvet
layer of its blossom.

Up a steep path
without footsteps
or a knock at the door
like a prayer that is answered,
it finds me.

And I know
even as I sleep
that some goodness
has come close,
here, where all
blessings find us,
unstartled and open-faced.[35]

Summary of the Four Renunciations

Christians follow "The Way" in imitation of Christ who revealed to us how to live our human lives as we return to God. On God's side we are blessed and endowed with deifying grace, which is full of love and light. On our side we respond by picking up our cross and following in the footsteps of those who have gone before us. In the monastic tradition we are instructed to undergo the four renunciations if we want to enjoy the contemplative life now and also in the next realm. This way of life is open to all contemplative seekers.

In the tradition, there are four renunciations. In the first renunciation we renounce our former way of life, which is characterized by the attachments of the ego, and, instead, we live selflessly a life of charity and working on behalf of our political, social, and interpersonal domains. We follow the gospel in serving the poor, sharing our goods, being faithful in friendships, commitments, work assignments, and engaging in dialogue globally. The world is treasured and there is a harmony in one's life arising from doing all things for the glory of God. Whenever we sin, we repent and ask for forgiveness and make amends. We worship with our faith community and contribute to the building up of society and the arts. The environment is safeguarded for the benefit of creation in all its forms.

In this first renunciation we renounce all that is not contributing to the building up of God's reign in the here and now. Our baptismal commitment is to return to those quickened waters in which we dissolve the false self and rise to the true self. Christ Jesus lives in us, and we unite not only in faith but also in actual graced living. This first renunciation is the journey above the river: doing good and avoiding evil.

In the second renunciation we take on the spiritual journey that is interior and under the river. This is to live our life from our depths and in tune with our motivations, our hidden desires, and passions. This second renunciation is to renounce the thoughts that, when unchecked, lead us down the slope toward our afflictions: the classic afflictive thoughts of food, sex, things, anger, dejection, acedia, vainglory, and pride. These afflictions take us away from our resolve, and soon we are back above the river and living as if we never plunged under the river on the journey of renouncing our former ways of life. Through the second renunciation, however, we gain peace of mind and learn the art and discipline of replacing our attachments with interior prayer and the poise of discernment.

In the third renunciation we renounce our self-made thoughts of God so we can know the God who is God. Our direct experience finds a language and story within our particular faith tradition. We refrain from projecting our particular credo on others, who have encountered a different faith tradition. But more than that, we refrain from projecting on God ideas of God that rise from ego consciousness. According to the monastic elders, we know that we can experience God when we lay aside our thoughts, any and all thoughts, feelings, passions. In emptiness we stand naked before God and the Presence springs up. This ineffable manifestation is accessed through our spiritual senses. We enter into the Mystery with our commitment to follow the directives of our own psychic imprint[36] of how faith has been planted deep in our hearts. We follow our initiation into a life of faith and fidelity to the encounter with revelation. We take off our shoes and kneel before the Mystery. We are mute. We practice unthinking and are known heart to heart. In silence and awe we adore the Holy One.

In the fourth renunciation we renounce the thoughts of our self. We accept the gift to leap from self-centeredness to sacrifice on behalf of others. Humility springs up, replacing attachment to ignorance, illusion, and greed. We treasure creation and celebrate life with our spiritual senses open, awake, and involved in the Mystery. Others call humility what they see of our purity of heart, as our silence deepens and we diminish the dynamic of self-reflexiveness. Purity of heart integrates the body, mind, and soul into a single harmonious being.

The images used in this book might assist us in ways of understanding the spiritual journey. I have used the metaphor of the river as the way we course toward God, and I have said that we can make our journey on the surface of the river or below in its depths. Above the river we make the external journey by doing good and avoiding evil, as in the first renunciation. Below the surface of the river we make the spiritual or hidden journey that no one sees, and indeed we cannot see ourselves. There we undergo the other three renunciations imperceptible to others who do not see our thoughts, motivations, and afflictions. We renounce the eight afflictions that initially arise as thoughts; then we refrain from self-made thoughts of God and finally from self-made thoughts of self. We use the term psychic imprint to denote the receptivity of our soul toward our vocation—our calling from God. The teachings are available, and our hearts are longing for this contemplative way of life. With this little book we follow in "The Way" that humble woman who received the Word, went to visit her cousin Elizabeth in haste, served her "yes" all the way to Calvary, and stood strong beneath the cross.

A Meditation on Kenosis[37]

Humility matters. Since ultimately God is our heart's desire, we long to be nothing for the sake of everything, in imitation of Christ who emptied himself that all may have life to the full. In this book we have taken a long look at how we can respond to grace in order to empty ourselves of all that is not God in imitation of Jesus. This journey is often called "The Way." From the monastic tradition we see that "The Way" leads through the low doors of humility. A strange paradox is our lot: To become humble is to embrace the human condition as it is and yet also to renounce attachments to any self-made illusions about that human condition. So comprehensive is this teaching that we may say that humility is for a Christian what enlightenment is for a Buddhist, realization for a Hindu, sincerity for a Confucian, righteousness for a Jew, surrender for a Muslim, and annihilation for a Sufi. Through the four renunciations we come to purity of heart: the face of humility.

I wrote this coda on humility on a bus while on pilgrimage in Turkey with a group of devout Muslims and Christians. We had just traced those ancient paths in Cappadocia where once lived Basil, his brother Gregory of Nyssa, his friend Gregory of Nazianzus, and all those early church elders who gave us language for this mystical life. They, like ourselves, must have pondered the provocative hymn that honors the humility of Christ found in the second chapter of the Apostle Paul's letter to the Philippians:

> Who, though he was in the form of God, did not regard equality with God as something to be grasped, but emptied himself, taking the form of a servant, being born in the likeness of men. And being found

in human form he humbled himself and became obedient unto death, even death on a cross.

> Therefore God also highly exalted him
> And gave him the name
> That is above every name,
> So that at the name of Jesus
> Every knee should bend,
> In heaven and on earth and under the earth,
> And every tongue should confess
> That Jesus Christ is Lord,
> To the glory of God the Father. (Phil 2:6–11)

The early Christians celebrated the paradox of Christ's divine self-surrender and found in it a supreme way to put on Christ. They sang a hymn in honor of Jesus' self-emptying, how he "humbled" himself of himself. The life of Jesus incarnates a way to become human by a path of self-renunciation, and our early spiritual ancestors sought to imitate him. This is the legacy of wisdom he and they offer us. It is not by striving for or clinging to some imagined divinity that we imitate Our Lord, but by becoming fully human by renouncing all that is not truly human. And so in imitation of Christ, we too can empty ourselves of ourselves and learn the way of humility. As it was in the beginning, is now, and ever shall be: humility matters.

Appendix 1

Was Jesus Angry?[38]

This question comes up so frequently and seems to justify anger among the best of us. The following is a *lectio*. Since anger, according to St. Basil, is the biggest obstacle to prayer, I've spent many months engaged in teachings about anger. I always return to John Cassian's admonition that the monk ought not be angry. Let's take a long look at Jesus driving out the money changers in the temple:

The scriptural accounts (Matthew 21; Mark 11; Luke 19; and John 2) give us several versions of this significant incident. The number of quotations from scripture about overcoming anger, hatred, violence, and murder seem to be lost to memory, as this one episode is quoted back to me every time I teach the thought of anger. So, let me linger here and give a context for and interpretation of this important event in Jesus' life.

The Synoptic Gospels place the event at the end of Jesus' life and ministry. These accounts differ somewhat in detail, but in general each of the three gospels present the cleansing of the temple as the immediate provocation leading ultimately to the crucifixion of Jesus.

In John's gospel, on the other hand, Jesus' cleansing of the temple is placed at the beginning of his public ministry, and it is described in much greater detail than in the Synoptic Gospels. This placement serves to foreshadow both Jesus' death and resurrection ("Destroy this temple and in three days I will raise it up"). In John's gospel it is the raising of Lazarus which is presented as bringing on the events that lead to Jesus' passion and death.

So, what are we to make of this violent outburst of Jesus? How does it square with Cassian's rigorous teaching on anger: "Our Lord and Savior . . . desired to remove completely the dregs of wrath from the inmost depths of the soul"? Cassian's instruction merely echoes Jesus' own uncompromising words, which suggest that anger is as serious an offense as murder. "You have heard that it was said to those of ancient time, 'You shall not murder'; and 'whoever murders shall be liable to judgment.' But I say to you 'that if you are angry with a brother or sister, you will be liable to judgment'" (Mt 5:21–22; *Conferences*, pp. 566–67).

Was Jesus angry? The brief accounts in the Synoptic Gospels give so little detail that it is plausible to imagine that Jesus' action was carried out with composure. In none of the gospel accounts does the narrative say that Jesus was angry. In fact, in Matthew's gospel it is the chief priests and scribes who are described as being angry.

The detailed description of Jesus in John's gospel weakens this argument somewhat, but it doesn't say he was angry. There Jesus fashions a whip and drives out the large animals destined for slaughter. After Jesus' death his disciples quote scripture to interpret Jesus' actions as that of a zealot. Clearly John's narrative provides a more vivid picture of Jesus' actions than do the Synoptics, a portrayal that reasonably could be interpreted as anger. But notice how he frees the birds, turns the tables, and strikes no one. He quotes scripture texts that would have been known to the officials, but harms no one.

What was the significance of Jesus' action? Maybe it is not that fruitful to ask about Jesus' emotional state during the cleansing of the temple. This is not a psychological text; it is a prophetic text. This sounds simplistic, but it's hard to overemphasize this point. There are vast resonances here with the biblical tradition of Israel, the Hebrew Scriptures. First, in this incident we have Jesus linked with a long line of prophetic actions in the history of Israel. Here are some examples:

Isaiah walks naked and barefoot for three years as a sign of the captivity of Egypt and Ethiopia to Assyria (Is 20:1–6), an image of the shame and defeat that await these two nations and a warning to those in Israel who want to seek security in alliance with military strength rather than seeking security in the Lord.

Jeremiah smashes an earthenware jug to symbolize the fate of Jerusalem if the people refuse to listen to the Lord and give up their idols (Jer 19:1–15).

Jeremiah wears a wooden yoke that symbolizes a willingness to obey the Lord and accept subjugation to Babylon (Jer 27 and 28). In exile Israel will be in a better position to restore its relationship with God. In a worldly sense, the exiles have lost everything, although these things were just illusions; stripped of these illusions, all they have left is the reality of a right relationship with God.

Ezekiel is instructed to enact a series of prophetic signs: he makes a clay map of Jerusalem and sets up a mock siege around it, warning the exiles not to hope for rescue from the doomed city. Ezekiel places an iron plate between himself and the map of the city representing the barrier of sin between the people and God. Ezekiel lies on his side for 430 days eating siege rations, symbolizing a people enfeebled by their sin. Ezekiel shaves his head and beard with a sword, the military instrument used in Jerusalem's defeat, symbolizing the humiliation in defeat and loss of vitality (Ezk 4 and 5).

Ezekiel is instructed to pack a bag and dig around a city wall to convince the exiles of the fate of those who remain in Jerusalem (Ezk 12).

Hosea's marriage to the prostitute Gomer is a prophetic symbol of the Lord's relationship to unfaithful Israel (Hos 3).

Thus, Jesus' behavior corresponds to other prophetic actions directed toward Israel, gestures that were sometimes peculiar and perplexing to those who observed them. Second, the meaning of Jesus' prophetic action is consistent with the message of the prophets who preceded him. In all three Synoptic Gospels Jesus accompanies his prophetic action with words from two prophetic texts—Isaiah (56:7) and Jeremiah (7:11). Thus, Jesus is prophet in both word and deed. Here are a few examples:

> The context of the quotation from Isaiah ("my house shall be called a house of prayer") emphasizes the universal vocation of Israel to draw all nations to the Lord (Gn 12: 2–3; Ex 19:5–6; Is 2:2–3; Zech 8:20–23), a vocation that Israel is failing to live out.

> The context of the quotation from Jeremiah ("you have made it a den of robbers") rebukes Israel for relying on the illusion that the presence of the temple itself is enough to sustain a relationship with God. The phrase "den of robbers" is often interpreted to mean that the commercial activity in the temple was corrupt. However, the "den of robbers" refers to the "hideout" of the robbers. In Jeremiah and in the Synoptic Gospels the reference is to those who seek to find security in the outward manifestation of religious activity and the temple. Sacrifices in the temple are meaningless without true and heartfelt devotion to God (Is 1:11–15; Jer 6:20; Amos 4:4–5; 5:21–25; Mic 6:6–8; Pss 40:6–8; 50:7–14; 51:16–17; 69:30–31).

> In Matthew and Mark, the cleansing of the temple is joined to the story of the withered fig tree, a further prophetic sign of Israel's lack of spiritual fruit. In the book of the prophet Hosea, there is a lovely image in which God compares finding the forebears of Israel to the delight of finding the first fruit of a fig tree (Hos 9:10). In Matthew, Jesus heals the blind and the lame after driving the buyers and sellers out of the temple, an allusion with messianic overtones to the restoration of Zion described in Is 35:5–6.

How do we interpret Jesus' actions in the light of the Old Testament, especially the prophetic tradition? Jesus' action in cleansing the temple is a protest like that of the prophets of old against the profanation of God's house and a sign that the messianic purification of the temple was at hand. With this interpretation we can see that Jesus empties the temple in order to make room for himself. The vehemence of Jesus' action indicates the beginning of a radical new order of worship.

These interpretations of Jesus' action in the cleansing of the temple point to the substance of this text. The text is not to be read as Jesus' teaching on anger; we have been given that in Matthew's version of the Sermon on the Mount (Mt 5:10–11). Rather, this text completes the prophetic vision of the Old Testament: The purpose of the temple has been fulfilled in Christ; in him we encounter the Lord, the God of Israel, and offer worship and praise.

In conclusion to this short study on Jesus' anger and Cassian's admonitions, I'd also like to say that the eight afflictions are not just isolated incidents, or the chill of reaction to adversity, but sustained, protracted, abiding moods that cover our consciousness. We all know the difference between a passing rise in blood pressure when we see someone taking advantage of a little one and we feel indignant and when we are in such a steady state of anger that we kick the cat and slam doors with no immediate provocation.

Jesus was and is human and has fully experienced the range of emotions. Scripture is a teaching about the significance of Jesus and a guide for our historical living as Christians. Anything that draws us away from purity of heart is not the intention of our sacred texts.

Appendix 2

Friends on the Spiritual Journey

Bonds of friendship sever when differences become irreconcilable. Humility provides the criteria when we need to part for the sake of our soul.

> Hence, as we have said, only the ties of a friendship which is founded upon similarity of virtuousness are trustworthy and indissoluble, for "the Lord makes those of one mind to dwell in the house." Therefore love can abide unbroken only in those in whom there is one chosen orientation and one desire, one willing and one not willing. If you also wish to preserve this inviolable, you must first strive, after having expelled your vices, to put to death your own will and with common earnestness and a common chosen orientation, to fulfill diligently what the prophet takes such great delight in: "Behold, how good and how pleasant it is for brothers to dwell in unity." This should be understood not in terms of place but spiritually. For it profits nothing if those who disagree about behavior and chosen orientation are together in one dwelling, nor is it a drawback to those who are of like virtue to be separated by distance. With God it is common behavior rather than a common location that joins brothers in a single dwelling, and the fullness of peace can never be maintained where there is a difference of wills. (Cassian, *Conferences,* p. 559)

There are many degrees of intimacy: parent for children, family, work associates, teachers and students. Friends are equals and the substance for the bond is spiritual agreement. The balance tips in favor of separation when friends not only do not share spiritual practice, but also when scorn is spoken toward the once treasured friend. Adversarial relationships might be in service of humility, when rightly suffered for the sake of a higher goal, but since friendship is to will and to refuse the same thing, contentiousness need not be tolerated.

Briefly, let's review the eight thoughts and note how friends keep each other faithful on the spiritual path:

> Eating the middle way
> Fasting and feasting in balance
> Hospitality honored.

> Practice celibacy according to vocation
> Chaste in mind
> Guard the heart
> Watching the thoughts.

> Things used in harmony with vocation
> Shared, reverenced, and in order
> Middle way preferred.

> Anger restrained
> When provoked
> seek forgiveness
> Anticipate.

> Dejection treated
> Acedia prevented
> Compunction received.

> Vain thoughts observed
> Glory given to God.

> Pride checked, curbed
> Consciously watching thoughts
> manifested in motivations
> Serving others egolessly.

Mystery honored
Prayer ceaseless
Cell for solitude, silence, and stillness
Friends break bread and wash feet.

In short, the friends coach each other along their spiritual journey. Anger divides friends and should not be tolerated. If a friend is a habitual occasion of sin, then part. What about fidelity? Can we squander our next life?

Is not friendship unconditional loving? The other's spiritual life is what is unconditional here. Friends are optional: pairing, freely bonding, and freely parting if the spiritual journey isn't shared. A question rises: Can there be friends that don't share a sense of God consciousness? Humility governs differences that do not divide, but at rock bottom, just as sin parts us from God on our side, so too do friends part when the spiritual journey is not shared.

Can this be a cause to leave the priesthood, religious life, or a marriage? Or is there priesthood, religious life, or a marriage without a spiritual bond "to will and refuse" the same thing? There is the honest recognition that there is nothing to leave, only something to find, a pearl of great price.

Appendix 3

Scripture for *Lectio* on the Eight Afflictions[39]

Thoughts about Food

Mt 9:15. And Jesus said to them, "The wedding guests cannot mourn as long as the bridegroom is with them, can they? The days will come when the bridegroom is taken away from them, and then they will fast."

Cassian uses the first part of the verse (bridegroom with them) to explain why a monk would break a fast when receiving guests.

Rom 14:10. Why do you pass judgment on your brother or sister? Or you, why do you despise your brother or sister? For we will all stand before the judgment seat of God?

Mt 7:1. Do not judge, so that you may not be judged. For with the judgment you make you will be judged, and the measure you give will be the measure you get.

Mt 4:2–4. ²He fasted forty days and forty nights, and afterwards he was famished. ³The tempter came and said to him, "If you are the Son of God, command these stones to become loaves of bread." ⁴But he answered, "It is written, 'One does not live by bread alone, but by every word that comes from the mouth of God.'"

Mt 11:18–19. ¹⁸For John came neither eating nor drinking, and they say, "He has a demon;" ¹⁹The Son of Man came eating and drinking, and they say, "Look, a glutton and a drunkard, a friend of tax collectors and sinners!" Yet wisdom is vindicated by her deeds.

Gn 1:29–30. ²⁹God said, "See, I have given you every plant yielding seed that is upon the face of all the earth, and every tree with seed in its fruit;

you shall have them for food. [30]And to every beast of the earth, and to every bird of the air, and to everything that creeps on the earth, everything that has the breath of life, I have given every green plant for food."

Gn 9:3. Every moving thing that lives shall be food for you; and just as I gave you the green plants, I give you everything.

Rom 14:3. Those who eat must not despise those who abstain, and those who abstain must not pass judgment on those who eat; for God has welcomed them.

Rom 14:17. For the kingdom of God is not food and drink but righteousness and peace and joy in the Holy Spirit.

1Cor 8:8. Food will not bring us closer to God. We are no worse off if we do not eat, nor are we better off if we do.

1Cor 8:13. Therefore, if food is a cause of their falling, I will never eat meat, so that I may not cause one of them to fall.

Rom 14:20. Do not for the sake of food, destroy the work of God. Everything is indeed clean, but it is wrong for you to make others fall by what you eat.

1Pt 4:11. Whoever speaks must do so as one speaking the very words of God; whoever serves must do so with the strength that God supplies, so that God may be glorified in all things through Jesus Christ. To him belong the glory and the power forever and ever. Amen

Rom 14:6. Those who observe the day, observe it in honor of the Lord. Also those who eat, eat in honor of the Lord, since they give thanks to God; while those who abstain, abstain in honor of the Lord and give thinks to God.

The advantages of moderation

Prv 21:17. Whoever loves pleasure will suffer want; whoever loves wine and oil will not be rich.

Prv 23:1–3. [1]When you sit down to eat with a ruler, observe carefully what is before you, [2]and put a knife to your throat if you have a big appetite. [3]Do not desire the ruler's delicacies, for they are deceptive food.

Prv 23:20–21. [20]Do not be among winebibbers, or among gluttonous eaters of meat; [21]for the drunkard and the glutton will come to poverty, and drowsiness will clothe them with rags.

Sir 31:19–20. How ample a little is for a well-disciplined person. He does not breathe heavily when in bed. Healthy sleep depends on moderate eating; he rises early, and feels fit. The distress of sleeplessness and of nausea and colic are with the glutton.

Sir 31:22. Listen to me, my child, and do not disregard me, and in the end you will appreciate my words. In everything you do be moderate, and no sickness will overtake you.

Sir 31:12–31. *Deals with moderation in food and drink.*

A true fast is inward

Jl 2:12–13. Yet even now says the LORD, return to me with all your heart, with fasting, with weeping, and with mourning; rend your hearts and not your clothing. Return to the LORD, your God, for he is gracious and merciful, slow to anger, and abounding in steadfast love, and relents from punishing.

Mt 6:16–18. And whenever you fast, do not look dismal, like the hypocrites, for they disfigure their faces so as to show others that they are fasting. Truly I tell you, they have received their reward. But when you fast, put oil on your head and wash your face, so that your fasting may be seen not by others but by your Father who is in secret; and your Father who sees in secret will reward you.

Lk 12:24. Consider the ravens: they neither sow nor reap, they have neither storehouse nor barn, and yet God feeds them. Of how much more value are you than the birds!

Nm 11:4–6. The rabble among them had a strong craving; and the Israelites also wept again, and said, "If only we had meat to eat! We remember the fish we used to eat in Egypt for nothing, the cucumbers, the melons, the leeks, the onions, and the garlic; but now our strength is dried up, and there is nothing at all but this manna to look at."

The irony and meaning in this text are not hard to detect, but if you look closely, repetition of the word "nothing" and the point of view expressed by the Israelites are keys to catching that meaning. These are some of the things to look for when trying to figure out more difficult texts. Their food in Egypt was hardly "for nothing"; they paid dearly in bondage to Pharaoh. And the "nothing at all" that they see as so unappealing is the bread of angels provided by the God who wants to sustain them in their journey to the Promised Land. If their strength is dried up it is not because God has not given them everything they need. Maybe it is a biblical example of acedia. (If you are interested, look at the next few verses following these. The narrator is pointing out that the manna is not all that bad—it is the ancient world's equivalent of Bisquick!)

Ps 22:27. The poor shall eat and be satisfied; those who seek him shall praise the LORD. May your hearts live forever.

Spiritual food

Is 55: 1–2. Lo, everyone who thirsts, come to the waters; and you that have no money, but come and eat! Come, buy wine and milk without money and without price. Why do you spend your money for that which is not bread, and your labor for that which does not satisfy: Listen carefully to me, and eat what is good, and delight yourselves in rich food.

Sir 24:19–20. [Lady Wisdom speaks:] ²⁹Come to me, you who desire me, and eat your fill of my fruits. ³⁰For the memory of me is sweeter than honey, and the possession of me sweeter than the honeycomb.

Jn 4:31–32. Meanwhile the disciples were urging him, "Rabbi, eat something." But he said to them, "I have food to eat that you do not know about."

Jn 6:26–27. Jesus answered them, "Very truly, I tell you, you are looking for me, not because you saw signs, but because you ate your fill of the loaves. Do not work for the food that perishes, but for the food that endures for eternal life, which the Son of Man will give to you. For it is on him that God the Father has set his seal."

Jn 6:55. For my flesh is true food and my blood is true drink.

Jn 6:58. This is the bread that came down from heaven, not like that which your ancestors ate, and they died. But the one who eats this bread will live forever.

Jn 19:28. After this, when Jesus knew that all was now finished, he said (in order to fulfill the scripture), "I am thirsty."

There really is not a neat division between God's provision of "physical" food and "spiritual" food. But we can get it mixed up—that's what Jesus is trying to point out in Jn 6:26–27. They ate and were physically satisfied, but they could not recognize and benefit from the spiritual nourishment present and offered by the Lord.

In terms of "thoughts about food," the practice might be to lay down a thought about "spiritual food" next to each (afflictive) food thought.

Thoughts about Sex

Mt 5:27–28. "You have heard that it was said, 'You shall not commit adultery.' But I say to you that everyone who looks at a woman with lust has already committed adultery with her in his heart."

1Cor 7:3–4. The husband should give to his wife her conjugal rights, and likewise the wife to her husband. For the wife does not have authority over her own body, but the husband does; likewise the husband does not have authority over his own body, but the wife does.

1Cor 6:13b. The body is meant not for fornication but for the Lord, and the Lord for the body.

1Cor 6:18. Shun fornication! Every sin that a person commits is outside the body but the fornicator sins against the body itself.

1Cor 6:19. Do you know that your body is a temple of the Holy Spirit within you, which you have from God, and that you are not your own?

1Thess 4:3. For this is the will of God, your sanctification: that you abstain from fornication; that each one of you knows how to control your own body in holiness and honor.

1Thess 4:7. For God did not call us to impurity but in holiness.

1Cor 7:8–9. To the unmarried and the widows I say that it is well for them to remain unmarried as I am. But if they are not practicing self-control, they should marry. For it is better to marry than to be aflame with passion.

This text brings some problems—it is one of those texts people would like to "modernize." I admit that I am uneasy about placing one state of life "above" another, but that is what the text says. It seems that the important point here is reflected later in the chapter (vv. 32–38). "We should embrace a way of life in which we are as free from anxiety as possible (vs. 32) and which promotes good order and unhindered devotion to the Lord (vs. 35)."

Mt 19:11–12. [Jesus] said to them, "Not everyone can accept this teaching, but only those to whom it is given. For there are eunuchs who have been so since birth, and there are eunuchs who have been made eunuchs by others, and there are eunuchs who have made themselves eunuchs for the sake of the kingdom of heaven. Let anyone accept this who can."

This verse complements the previous verse from Paul and religious celibacy is a gift that calls for a response.

Phil 4:8. Finally, beloved, whatever is true, whatever is honorable, whatever is just, whatever is pure, whatever is pleasing, whatever is commendable, if there is any excellence and if there is anything worthy of praise, think about these things.

Sir 23:4–6. O Lord, Father and God of my life, do not give me haughty eyes, and remove evil desire from me. Let neither gluttony nor lust overcome me, and do not give me over to shameless passion.

Prv 4:23. Keep your heart with all vigilance, for from it flow the springs of life.

Heb 10:19–22. Therefore, my friends, since we have confidence to enter the sanctuary by the blood of Jesus, by the new and living way that he opened for us through the curtain (that is, through his flesh), and since we have a great priest over the house of God, let us approach with a true heart in full assurance of faith, with our hearts sprinkled clean from an evil conscience and our bodies washed with pure water.

Right effort

Ps 51. *What is especially appropriate is that the heading of the psalm gives its occasion as: "A Psalm of David, when the prophet Nathan came to him, after he had gone into Bathsheba." Surely this psalm is a gift to those with this affliction. (These headings are omitted in many printed versions of the Bible.)*

Ps 51:1. Have mercy on me, O God, according to your steadfast love; according to your abundant mercy blot out my transgressions.

Ps 51:2. Wash me thoroughly from my iniquity, and cleanse me from my sin.

Ps 51:10. Create in me a clean heart, O God, and put a new and right spirit within me.

Ps 51:17. The sacrifice acceptable to God is a broken spirit; a broken and contrite heart you will not despise.

Nakedness before God

Biblical imagery of nakedness is a negative one. Nakedness is a reflection of our vulnerability, yes, but the emphasis is on sin, the separation from God that caused the vulnerability in the first place. Hence, nakedness = sinful-ness, brokenness. In terms of biblical language, to stand naked before God is to stand in fear, shame and judgment; it is not an image of docility or sur-render (although later spiritual writing may have come to use the imagery in that way).

Therefore, God's desire is to clothe us, to cover our nakedness and heal our vulnerability. It seemed to me that in addition to the Genesis reference, it would be good to suggest a passage or two which uses nuptial imagery for our destiny with God and speaks of humanity being clothed in the wedding garments which symbolize the restoration of full and free intimacy with God. (Marital love between a man and woman is faint image of the love between God and humanity—not the other way around—and that may be why Paul says remaining unmarried is better.)

Gn 3:9–10. But the LORD God called to the man, and said to him, "Where are you?" He said, "I heard the sound of you in the garden, and I was afraid, because I was naked; and I hid myself."

Is 61:10. I will greatly rejoice in the LORD, my whole being shall exult in my God; for he has clothed me with garments of salvation, he has covered me with the robe of righteousness, as a bridegroom decks himself with a garland, and as a bride adorns herself with her jewels.

Rv 19:7–8. "Let us rejoice and exult and give him the glory, for the marriage of the Lamb has come, and his bride has made herself ready; to her it has been granted to be clothed with fine linen bright and pure"—for the fine linen is the righteous deeds of the saints.

Thoughts about Things

Lk 14:28–33. [28]"For which of you, intending to build a tower, does not first sit down and estimate the cost to see whether he has enough to complete it? [29]Otherwise, when he has laid a foundation and is not able to finish, all who see it will begin to ridicule him, saying, 'This fellow began to build and was not able to finish.'

[31]Or what king, going out to wage war against another king, will not sit down first and consider whether he is able with ten thousand to oppose the one who comes against him with twenty thousand?

[32]If he cannot, then, while the other is still far away, he sends a delegation and asks for the terms of peace. [33]So therefore, none of you can become my disciple if you do not give up all your possessions."

Cassian refers to vv. 31 and 32 to make the point that it is better not to make the (monastic?) renunciation if one is not going to follow through with that renunciation.

Mt 6:24. "No one can serve two masters; for a slave will either hate the one and love the other, or be devoted to the one and despise the other. You cannot serve God and wealth."

Mt 19:16–22. ¹⁶Then someone came to him and said, "Teacher, what good deed must I do to have eternal life?" ¹⁷And he said to him, "Why do you ask me about what is good? There is only one who is good. If you wish to enter into life, keep the commandments." ¹⁸He said to him, "Which ones?" And Jesus said, "You shall not murder. You shall not steal. You shall not bear false witness. ¹⁹Honor your father and mother. Also, you shall love your neighbor as yourself." ²⁰The young man said to him, "I have kept all these; what do I still lack?" ²¹Jesus said to him, "If you wish to be perfect, go sell your possessions, and give the money to the poor, and you will have treasure in heaven; then come, follow me." ²²When the young man heard this word, he went away grieving, for he had many possessions.

Mk 13:14–16. But when you see the desolating sacrilege set up where it ought not to be (let the reader understand), then those in Judea must flee to the mountains; ¹⁵the one on the housetop must not go down or enter the house to take anything away; ¹⁶the one in the field must not turn back to get a coat.

Mt 26:14–16. Then one of the twelve, who was called Judas Iscariot, went to the chief priests and said, "What will you give me if I betray him to you?" They paid him thirty pieces of silver. And from that moment he began to look for an opportunity to betray him.

2Kgs 5:1–27. *This chapter is the story of Naaman the Syrian, Elisha, and Gehazi. It is a long reference, but the nice thing about the whole story is that it shows Naaman finding out that he does not need to buy the favor of the God of Israel and Elisha as an exemplary prophet who does not seek personal gain as a servant of the LORD. Gehazi is an example of covetousness in seeking to acquire wealth that he never had.*

Acts 5:1–11. *The story of Ananias and Sapphira. There is an example of covetousness in holding on to part of what they had claimed to give up.*

Acts 4:32–37. *This is about possessions among the first Christians and the specific example of Barnabas. It is the "prologue" to the troubling story of Ananias and Sapphira. Both stories read together present the choice of the "two ways" to be a believer: Do you want to follow the path which Barnabas has taken that leads to life or the path which Ananias and Sapphira have chosen that leads to death? (Cf. Psalm 1)*

Rom 15:25–27. ²⁵At present, however, I am going to Jerusalem in a ministry to the saints; ²⁶for Macedonia and Achaia have been pleased to share their resources with the poor among the saints at Jerusalem. ²⁷They were pleased to do this, and indeed they owe it to them; for if the Gentiles have come to share in their spiritual blessings, they ought also to be of service to them in material things.

1Tm 6:6–10. ⁶Of course, there is great gain in godliness combined with contentment; ⁷for we brought nothing into the world, so that we can take nothing out of it; ⁸but if we have food and clothing, we will be content with these. ⁹But those who want to be rich fall into temptation and are trapped by many senseless and harmful desires that plunge people into ruin and destruction. ¹⁰For the love of money is a root of all kinds of evil, and in their eagerness to be rich some have wandered away from the faith and pierced themselves with many pains.

Eccl 5.10. The lover of money will not be satisfied with money; nor the lover of wealth with gain. This also is vanity.

1Tm 6:17–19. ¹⁷As for those who in the present age are rich, command them not to be haughty, or to set their hopes on the uncertainty of riches, but rather of God who richly provides us with everything for our enjoyment. ¹⁸They are to do good, to be rich in good works, generous, and ready to share, ¹⁹thus storing up for themselves the treasure of a good foundation for the future, so that they may take hold of the life that really is life.

Lk 21:1–4. [Jesus] looked up and saw rich people putting their gifts into the treasury; he also saw a poor widow put in two small copper coins. He said "Truly I tell you this poor widow has put in more than all of them; for all of them have contributed out of their abundance, but she out of her poverty has put in all she had to live on."

Lk 21:5–6. When some were speaking about the temple, how it was adorned with beautiful stones and gifts dedicated to God, he said, "As for these things that you see, the days will come when not one stone will be left upon another, all will be thrown down."

Ex 35:1–35 and 36:1–7. *The tabernacle was God's idea and the people responded with a willing heart (notice how many times that idea is repeated) and so much generosity that they finally had to be told to stop bringing* offerings! *The temple, on the other hand, never was the same as the taber-nacle; it was not God's idea (2 Sm 7:1–7). And the people continually con-fused the means with the end; they mistakenly thought that as long as they had the temple they could be assured of God's presence with them (Jer 7:1–7).*

Acts 3:1–10. *This is the story of Peter at the gate of the temple. "I have no silver and gold, but what I have I give you."*

Thoughts of Anger

Mt 5:22. "But I say to you that if you are angry with a brother or sister, you will be liable to judgment."

Mt 5:23–24. "So when you are offering your gift at the altar, if you remem-ber that your brother or sister has something against you, leave your gift there before the altar and go; first be reconciled to your brother or sister, and then come and offer your gift."

Eph 4:26–27. [26]Be angry but do not sin; do not let the sun go down on your anger, [27]and do not make room for the devil.

Ps 4:4. When you are disturbed, do not sin; ponder it on your beds, and be silent.

Eph 4:31–32. [31]Put away from you all bitterness and wrath and anger and wrangling and slander, together with all malice, [32] and be kind to one an-other, tender-hearted, forgiving one another as God in Christ has forgiven you.

1Tm 2:8. I desire then, that in every place the men should pray, lifting up holy hands without anger or argument.

1Jn 3:15. All who hate a brother or sister are murderers, and you know that murderers do not have eternal life abiding in them.

Lv 19:17–18. [17]You shall not hate in your heart anyone of your kin; you shall reprove your neighbor, or you will incur guilt yourself. [18]You shall not take vengeance or bear a grudge against any of your people, but you shall love your neighbor as yourself; I am the LORD.

Jn 13:34. I give you a new commandment, that you love one another. Just as I have loved you, you also should love one another.

Jas 1:20. For your anger does not produce God's righteousness.

Eccl 7:9. Do not be quick to anger, for anger lodges in the bosom of fools.

Prv 14:17. One who is quick-tempered acts foolishly, and the schemer is hated.

Prv 29:22. One given to anger stirs up strife, and a hothead causes much transgression.

Mt 7:1–5. *This is about seeing the specks in other's eyes while ignoring the log in our own.*

Ps 37:8. Refrain from anger, and forsake wrath. Do not fret—it leads only to evil.

Prv 15:18. Those who are hot-tempered stir up strife, but those who are slow to anger calm contention.

Sir 28:1–13. *This is a lengthy section on anger and quarreling. There is one verse that I thought was interesting because it is consistent with the practice of replacing one thought with another. I suppose this could be interpreted "legalistically," as though God is a Divine Enforcer, but the whole point of the Law was to help Israel to be the kind of people God intended so they could accomplish the purpose for which they were created—to bring all nations, all people to knowledge and love of God. It all started with Abraham (Gn 12:2–3) and the covenants and commandments that followed were all part of God's faithfulness in keeping that promise to Abraham. Keeping the law is not for its own sake, but for the sake of the world. Israel's fidelity to the law would be a testimony to the nations and this would spark their desire to know God and his ways as Israel does. This is the sort of background that can enrich these seemingly legalistic passages—remembering the commandment means remembering God's desire to restore all of humanity to himself, it means remembering God's fidelity despite our infidelity, it means seeking to fulfill God's purpose in our lives.*

Sir 28:7. ⁷Remember the commandments, and do not be angry with your neighbor; remember the covenant of the Most High, and overlook faults.

Lk 22:50–51. ⁵⁰Then one of them struck the slave of the high priest and cut off his right ear. ⁵¹But Jesus said "No more of this!" And he touched his ear and healed him.

Mt 26:53–54. ⁵³"Do you think that I cannot appeal to my Father, and he will at once send me more than twelve legions of angels?"
⁵⁴"But how then would the scriptures be fulfilled, which say it must happen in this way?"

Mk 15:3–5. ³Then the chief priests accused him of many things. Pilate asked him again, "Have you no answer? See how many charges they bring against you." But Jesus made no further reply, so that Pilate was amazed.

Is 53:4–6. ⁴Surely he has borne our infirmities and carried our diseases; yet we accounted him stricken, struck down by God and afflicted. ⁵But he was wounded for our transgressions crushed for our iniquities; upon him was the punishment that made us whole, and by his bruises we are healed. ⁶All we like sheep have gone astray; we have turned to our own way, and the LORD has laid on him the iniquity of us all.

Lk 23:34. Then Jesus said, "Father, forgive them; for they do not know what they are doing."

Gn 45:5, 24. *Joseph tells his brothers not to be angry with themselves. Later, when they are taking leave to go home and tell their father that Joseph is alive, he tells his brothers not to quarrel along the way. Jacob welcomed the news and made plans to travel to Egypt to meet his lost son, Joseph. This is a parallel to the parable of the lost son (Lk 15:11). Neither father was angry.*

Thoughts of Dejection

Prv 25:20. Like vinegar on a wound is one who sings songs to a heavy heart. Like a moth in clothing or a worm in wood, sorrow gnaws at the human heart.

2 Cor 7:10. For godly grief produces a repentance that leads to salvation and brings no regret, but worldly grief produces death.

Jb 5:23. For you shall be in league with the stones of the field, and the wild animals shall be at peace with you.

Ps 119:165. Great peace have those who love your law; nothing can make them stumble.

Gal 5:22–23. By contrast, the fruit of the Spirit is love, joy, peace, patience, kindness, generosity, faithfulness, gentleness, and self-control. There is no law against these things.

Gn 4: 6–7, 14–15. ⁶The LORD said to Cain, "Why are you angry, and why has countenance fallen? If you do well, will you not be accepted? ⁷And if you do not do well, sin is lurking at the door; its desire is for you, but you must master it . . .' ¹⁴Today you have driven me away from the soil, and I shall be hidden from your face; I shall be a fugitive and a wanderer on the earth, and anyone who meets me may kill me." Then the LORD said to

him, "Not so! Whoever kills Cain will suffer a seven-fold vengeance."
¹⁵And the LORD put a mark on Cain, so that no one who came upon him would kill him.

From Cain's point of view he has a right to be angry because his offering has been rejected. (Why is it rejected? God never rejects an offering because of the nature of the offering, but because of the nature of the intention—the heart—of the one making the offering.) God's point of view, his response, is, I want to accept your offering; work on changing your heart toward your brother. God can read hearts and knows the animosity Cain has towards Abel. As readers we find out about the animosity in the following verses when it is acted out in Cain's murder of Abel. God is working in Cain's best interest by warning him that he is in danger of falling into sin and telling him that he can master the situation.

Cain does not respond to God's warning, however. Does God give up on Cain? No. Cain's response shows his point of view—despair. His punishment is more than he can take. He thinks God is abandoning him and that everyone he meets is going to be like him (talk about projection!) and kill him just like he killed his brother! That is the kind of world he sees himself living in. (What could he have done instead of despairing? Ask for forgiveness.) What is God's response? "Not so!" God will not abandon Cain; he has hardly hidden his face from him. Notice that the mark is one of protection, a reminder (to Cain, especially) of God's continued interest in Cain's welfare. This is the "vengeance" that God visits on Cain—reaching out to Cain and showing him that he wants to protect Cain, not in the least, from himself.

Notice, too, that God is speaking to Cain "face-to-face," so to speak. As the Genesis story progresses this kind of intimate conversation occurs less and less often. (I do not believe he ever speaks directly to Joseph at all. Quite a contrast to the lengthy conversations between God and Abraham!) This is a way that the narrative conveys humanity's movement further and further away from the ideal of walking with God in the Garden. (This is also a way to interpret the declining longevity in the Genesis narrative: the life span decreases as humanity moves further and further away from immortality.)

So Cain's point of view is that God is unfair, demanding, and dispenses unreasonable punishment. From God's point of view Cain's weaknesses are a threat to himself and others; God is trying to help him overcome them, assuring him of His presence and concern for his welfare. The key to reading the Bible is to always make the presupposition that God is acting in the best interest of humanity. God does not act capriciously or vindictively (contrary to what Cain and a lot of us sometimes think). The whole purpose of the Bible is to shift us from Cain's point of view and help us to see God's point of view—and then to take it as our own, so we can walk with God through the world of time like Enoch did (Gn 5:24) until God takes us back to the Garden (Gn 2:15).

Mt 27:3–5. ³When Judas, his betrayer, saw that Jesus was condemned, he repented and brought back the thirty pieces of silver to the chief priests and the elders. ⁴He said, "I have sinned by betraying innocent blood." But they said, "What is that to us? See to it yourself." ⁵Throwing down the pieces of silver in the temple, he departed; and he went and hanged himself.

There are some who read this as Judas acknowledging what he did. He would not likely have killed himself if he had really experienced God's forgiveness. I wonder if part of the point here is the callous response of the religious officials, illustrating their inability to manifest God's forgiveness. I do not know what to think of it.

Mt 26:75. Then Peter remembered what Jesus had said: "Before the cock crows, you will deny me three times." And he went out and wept bitterly.

Godly sorrow

Acts 3:19. Repent therefore, and turn to God so that your sins may be wiped out.

Ps 42:11. Why are you cast down, O my soul, and why are you disquieted within me? Hope in God; for I shall again praise him, my help and my God.

Jer 31:13. Then shall the young women rejoice in the dance, and the young men and the old shall be merry. I will turn their mourning into joy, I will comfort them, and give them gladness for sorrow.

Ps 11:12. You have turned my mourning into dancing; you have taken off my sackcloth and clothed me with joy.

Prv 17:22. A cheerful heart is good medicine, but a downcast spirit dries up the bones.

Ps 139:11–12. ¹¹If I say, "Surely the darkness shall cover me, and the light around me become night," ¹²even the darkness is not dark to you; the night is as bright as the day, for darkness is a light to you.

Jn 1:5. The light shines in the darkness, and the darkness did not overcome it.

Is 9:2. The people who walked in darkness have seen a great light; those who lived in a land of deep darkness—on them light has shined.

Thoughts of Acedia

Ps 91:5–6. You will not fear the terror of the night, or the arrow that flies by day, or the pestilence that stalks in darkness or the destruction that wastes at noonday.

2 Tm 2:4. No one serving in the army gets entangled in everyday affairs; the soldier's aim is to please the enlisting officer.

Ps 119:28. My soul melts away for sorrow; strengthen me according to your word.

1 Thes 4:9–12. ⁹Now concerning love of the brothers and sisters you do not need to have anyone write to you, for you yourselves have been taught by God to love one another; ¹⁰ and indeed you do love all the brothers and sisters throughout Macedonia. But we urge you, beloved, to do so more and more, ¹¹to aspire to live quietly, to mind your own affairs, and to work with your hands, as we directed you, ¹²so that you may behave properly toward outsiders and be dependent on no one.

2 Thes 3:6. Now we command you, beloved, in the name of our Lord Jesus Christ, to keep away from believers who are living in idleness and not according to the tradition that they received from us.

2 Thes 3:8–15. . . . ⁸and we did not eat anyone's bread without paying for it; but with toil and labor we worked night and day, so that we might not burden any of you. ⁹This was not because we do not have that right, but in order to give you an example to imitate. ¹⁰For even when we were with you, we gave you this command: Anyone unwilling to work should not eat. ¹¹For we hear that some of you are living in idleness, mere busybodies, not doing any work.

¹²Now such persons we command and exhort in the Lord Jesus Christ to do their work quietly and earn their own living. ¹³Brothers and sisters, do not be weary in doing what is right. ¹⁴Take note of those who do not obey what we say in this letter; have nothing to do with them, so that they may be ashamed. ¹⁵Do not regard them as enemies, but warn them as believers.

Eph 4:28. Thieves must give up stealing; rather let them labor and work honestly with their own hands, so as to have something to share with the needy.

Acts 20:33–35. I coveted no one's silver or gold or clothing. You know for yourselves that I worked with my own hands to support myself and my companions. In all this I have given you an example that by such work we must support the weak, remembering the words of the Lord Jesus, for he himself said, "It is more blessed to give than to receive."

Sir 33:28–29. [28]Put him to work, in order that he may not be idle, [29]for idleness teaches much evil.

1Cor 15:33. Do not be deceived: "Bad company ruins good morals."

Prv 28:19. Anyone who tills the land will have plenty of bread, but one who follows worthless pursuits will have plenty of poverty

Prv 23:21. For the drunkard and the glutton will come to poverty, and drowsiness will clothe them with rags.

Sleep/weariness

Lk 22: 45–46. When he got up from prayer, he came to the disciples and found them sleeping because of grief, and he said to them, "Why are you sleeping? Get up and pray that you may not come into the time of trial."

Mk 13:35–37. [35]Therefore, keep awake—for you do not know when the master of the house will come, in the evening, or at midnight, or at cock-crow, or at dawn, [36]or else he may find you asleep when he comes suddenly. [37]And what I say to you I say to all: Keep awake.

Rom 13:11–12. [11]Besides this, you know what time it is, how it is now the moment for you to wake from sleep. For salvation is nearer to us now than when we became believers; [12]the night is far gone, the day is near. Let us then lay aside the works of darkness and put on the armor of light.

Lk 8:15. But as for that in the good soil, these are the ones who, when they hear the word, hold it fast in an honest and good heart, and bear fruit with patient endurance.

Lk 21:19. By your endurance you will gain your souls.

Rom 15:4. For whatever was written in former days was written for our instruction, so that by steadfastness and by the encouragement of the scriptures we might have hope.

Heb 10:36–39. [36]For you need endurance, so that when you have done the will of God, you may receive what was promised. [37]For yet "in a little while, the one who is coming will come and will not delay; [38]but my righteous one will live by faith. My soul takes no pleasure in anyone who shrinks back." [39]But we are not among those who shrink back and so are lost, but among those who have faith and so are saved.

Heb 12:1. Therefore, since we are surrounded by so great a cloud of witnesses, let us also lay aside every weight and the sin that clings so closely, and let us run with perseverance the race that is set before us.

Taciturnity

Mt 12:36–37. ³⁶I tell you, on the day of judgment you will have to give an account for every careless word you utter; ³⁷for by your words you will be justified, and by your words you will be condemned.

Silence as a practice helps one to recognize why Jesus would have said such a thing. Imagine what the world would be like if people exercised mindfulness in their speech, or even just tried. And notice, too, that words have the power to give life. The importance of discernment is implied in this passage also.

Prv 11:12. Whoever belittles another lacks sense, but an intelligent person remains silent.

Prv 15:4. A gentle tongue is a tree of life, but perverseness in it breaks the spirit.

Prv 21:23. To watch over mouth and tongue is to keep out of trouble.

Prv 14:23. In all toil there is profit, but mere talk leads only to poverty.

Compunction

Lk 15:11–32. *This is the reference for the prodigal son in Luke—an illustration of compunction, especially vv. 17–23 beginning with the young man "coming to himself" and ending with the celebration called for by the father.*

Acts. 3:19. Repent therefore, and turn to God so that your sins may be wiped out.

Fear of the Lord

Prv 9:10. The fear of the LORD is the beginning of wisdom, and the knowledge of the Holy One is insight.

Prv 14:27. The fear of the LORD is a fountain of life, so that one may avoid the snares of death.

Prv 19:23. The fear of the LORD is life indeed; filled with it one rests secure and suffers no harm.

Ps 19:9. The fear of the LORD is pure enduring forever; the ordinances of the LORD are true and righteous altogether.

Ps 34:7–9. ⁷The angel of the LORD encamps around those who fear him, and delivers them. ⁸O taste and see that the LORD is good; happy are those who take refuge in him. ⁹O fear the LORD, you his holy ones, for those who fear him have no want. The young lions suffer want and hunger, but those who seek the LORD lack no good thing.

Ps 115:11. You who fear the LORD, trust in the LORD! He is their help and their shield.

Labor

Ps 90:17. Let the favor of the LORD our God be upon us, and prosper for us the work of our hands—O prosper the work of our hands!

Thoughts of Vainglory

Jn 5:44. How can you believe when you accept glory from one another and do not seek the glory that comes from the one who alone is God?

Gal 5:26. Let us not become conceited, competing against one another, envying one another.

Prv 4:27. Do not swerve to the right or to the left; turn your foot away from evil.

2 Cor 6:7–8. . . . ⁷with the weapons of righteousness for the right hand and for the left; ⁸in honor and dishonor, in ill repute and good repute . . .

Phil 3:19. Their end is destruction; their god is the belly; and their glory is in their shame; their minds are set on earthly things.

Ps 53:6. There they shall be in great terror, in terror such as has not been. For god will scatter the bones of the ungodly; they will be put to shame, for God has rejected them.

True glory

Rom 3:23. . . . all have sinned and fall short of the glory of God. . . .

1Cor 10:31. So, whether you eat or drink, or whatever you do, do everything for the glory of God.

Eph 3:20. Now to him who by the power at work within us is able to accomplish abundantly far more than all we can ask or imagine, to him be glory in the church and in Christ Jesus to all generations, forever and ever. Amen

1Pt 4:11. Whoever speaks must do so as one speaking the very words of God; whoever serves must do so with the strength that God supplies, so that God may be glorified in all things through Jesus Christ. To him belong the glory and the power forever and ever Amen.

Ps 115:1. Not to us. O LORD, not to us, but to your name give glory, for the sake of your steadfast love and faithfulness.

Is 6:1–8. ¹In the year that King Uzziah died, I saw the Lord sitting on a throne, high and lofty; and the hem of his robe filled the temple. ²Seraphs were in attendance above him; each had six wings: with two they covered their faces, and with two they covered their feet, and with two they flew. ³And one called to another and said: "Holy, holy, holy is the LORD of hosts; the whole earth is full of his glory." ⁴The pivots on the thresholds shook at the voices of those who called, and the house filled with smoke. ⁵And I said: "Woe is me! I am lost, for I am a man of unclean lips, and I live among a people of unclean lips; yet my eyes have seen the King the LORD of hosts!" ⁶Then one of the seraphs flew to me, holding a live coal that had been taken from the altar with a pair of tongs. ⁷The seraph touched my mouth with it and said: "Now that this has touched your lips, your guilt has departed and your sin is blotted out." ⁸Then I heard the voice of the Lord saying, "Whom shall I send, and who will go for us?" And I said, "Here am I; send me!"

Attribute all goodness to God

Is 26:12. O LORD, you will ordain peace for us, for indeed, all that we have done, you have done for us.

Ps 16:2. I say to the LORD, "You are my Lord; I have no good apart from you."

Lk 18:18–19. A certain ruler asked [Jesus], "God Teacher, what must I do to inherit eternal life?" Jesus said to him, "Why do you call me good? No one is good but God alone."

Concern for what others think/motivation

Mt 6:1–4. ¹Beware of practicing your piety before others in order to be seen by them; for then you have no reward from your Father in heaven. ²So whenever you give alms, do not sound a trumpet before you, as the hypocrites do in the synagogues and in the streets, so that they may be praised by others. Truly I tell you, they have received their reward. ³But when you give alms, do not let your left hand know what your right hand is doing, ⁴so that your alms may be done in secret; and your Father who sees in secret will reward you.

Mt 6:5–6. ⁵And whenever you pray, do not be like the hypocrites, for they love to stand and pray in the synagogues and at the street corners, so that they may be seen by others. Truly I tell you they have received their reward. But whenever you pray, go into your room and shut the door and pray to your Father who is in secret; and your Father who sees in secret will reward you.

Mt 6:16–18. ¹⁶ And whenever you fast, do not look dismal, like the hypocrites, for they disfigure their faces so as to show others that they are fasting. Truly I tell you they have received their reward.

⁷But when you fast, put oil on your head and wash your face, ¹⁸so that your fasting may be seen not by others but by your Father who is in secret; and your Father who sees in secret will reward you.

Mt 23:5–12. ⁵[The Pharisees] do all their deeds to be seen by others; for they make their phylacteries broad and their fringes long. ⁶They love to have the place of honor at banquets and the best seats in the synagogues, ⁷and to be greeted with respect in the marketplaces, and to have people call them rabbi. ⁸But you are not to be called rabbi for you have one teacher, and you are all the students. ⁹And call no one your father on earth, for you have one Father—the one in heaven. ¹⁰Nor are you to be called instructors, for you have one instructor, the Messiah. ¹¹The greatest among you will be your servant. ¹²All who exalt themselves will be humbled, and all who humble themselves will be exalted.

Lk 14:7–11. ⁷When [Jesus] noticed how the guests chose the places of honor, he told them a parable. ⁸When you are invited by someone to a wedding banquet, do not sit down at the place of honor, in case someone more distinguished than you has been invited by your host; ⁹and the host who invited both of you may come and say to you, 'give this person your place,' and then in disgrace you would start to take the lowest place. ¹⁰But when you are invited, go and sit down at the lowest place, so that when your host comes, he may say to you, 'Friend, move up higher'; Then you will be honored in the presence of all who sit at the table with you. ¹¹For all who exalt themselves will be humbled, and those who humble themselves will be exalted."

Lk 14:12–14. ¹² [Jesus] said also to the one who had invited him, "When you give a luncheon or a dinner, do not invite your friends or your brothers or your relatives or rich neighbors, in case they may invite you in return, and you would be repaid. ¹³But when you give a banquet, invite the poor, the crippled, the lame, and the blind. ¹⁴And you will be blessed because they cannot repay you, for you will be repaid at the resurrection of the righteous."

Rom 11:33–12:3. ³³O the depth of the riches and wisdom and knowledge of God. How unsearchable are his judgments and how inscrutable his ways! ³⁴"For who has known the mind of the Lord? ³⁵Or who has given a gift to him, to receive a gift in return? Who has been his counselor?" ³⁶For from him and through him and to him are all things. To him be the glory forever. Amen. –¹I appeal to you therefore, brothers and sisters, by the mercies of God, to present your bodies as a living sacrifice, holy and acceptable to God, which is your spiritual worship. ²Do not be conformed to this world, but be transformed by the renewing of your minds, so that you may discern what is the will of God—what is good and acceptable and perfect. ³For by the grace given to me I say to everyone among you not to think of yourself more highly than you ought to think, but to think with sober judgment, each according to the measure of faith that God has assigned.

Ps 51:6. You desire truth in the inward being; therefore teach me wisdom in my secret heart.

False spirituality

Col 2:16–23. ¹⁶Therefore do not let anyone condemn you in matters of food and drink or of observing festivals, new moons, or Sabbaths. ¹⁷These are only a shadow of what is to come, but the substance belongs to Christ. ¹⁸Do not let anyone disqualify you, insisting on self-abasement and worship of angels, dwelling on visions, puffed up without cause by a human way of thinking, ¹⁹and not holding fast to the head, from whom the whole body, nourished and held together by its ligaments and sinews, grows with a growth that is from God. ²⁰If with Christ you died to the elemental spirits of the universe, why do you live as if you still belonged to the world? Why do you submit to regulations, ²¹"Do not handle, Do not taste, Do not touch?" ²²All these regulations refer to things that perish with us; they are simply human commands and teachings. ²³These have indeed an appearance of wisdom in promoting self-imposed piety, humility, and severe treatment of the body, but they are of no value in checking self-indulgence.

Thoughts of Pride

Is 14:13–14. [13]You said in your heart, "I will ascend to heaven; I will raise my throne above the stars of God; I will sit on the mount of assembly on the heights of Zahphon; [14]I will ascend to the tops of the clouds, I will make myself like the Most High."

Gn 3:4–5. But the serpent said to the woman, "You will not die; for God knows that when you eat of it your eyes will be opened, and you will be like God, knowing good and evil."

Ps 52:7–9. [5]But God will break you down forever; he will snatch and tear you from your tent; he will uproot you from the land of the living. [6]The righteous will see, and fear, and will laugh at the evildoer, saying, "See the one who would not take refuge in God, but trusted in abundant riches, and sought refuge in wealth!"

Ps 131:1. O LORD, my heart is not lifted up, my eyes are not raised too high; I do not occupy myself with things too great and too marvelous for me.

Ps 36:12. Do not let the foot of the arrogant tread on me, or the hand of the wicked drive me away.

Jas 4:6. But he gives all the more grace; therefore it says, "God opposes the proud, but gives grace to the humble."

Prv 16:5. All those who are arrogant are an abomination to the LORD; be assured, they will not go unpunished.

The following sets of verses are "pairs of opposites" that Cassian uses as illustrations of how God restores humility to those who have been destroyed by pride.

Is 14:13a. I will ascend to heaven.

Ps 44:25. For we sink down to the dust.

Is 14:14b. I will make myself like the Most High.

Phil 2:6–8. . . . [6]though he was in the form of God . . . [7] he emptied himself and took the form of a slave . . . [8]he humbled himself and became obedient to the point of death. . . .

Is 14:13b. I will raise my throne above the stars of God.

Mt 11:29b. . . . learn from me; for I am gentle and humble in heart. . . .

Ex 5:2b. I do not know the LORD, and I will not let Israel go.

Jn 8:55. . . . If I would say that I do not know him, I would be a liar like you. But I do know him and I keep his word.

Ez 29:3b. My Nile is my own; I made it for myself.

Jn 5:30 and 14:10. I can do nothing on my own (Jn 5:30a). The Father who dwells in me does his works (Jn 14:10c).

Lk 4:6b. To you I will give their glory and all this authority; for it has been given over to me, and I give it to anyone I please.

2 Cor 8:9b. . . . though he was rich, yet for your sakes he became poor, so that by his poverty you might become rich.

Is 10:14b,c. . . . as one gathers eggs that have been forsaken, so I have gathered all the earth; and there was none that moved a wing or opened its mouth, or chirped.

Ps 102:7–8. I am like an owl of the wilderness . . . I lie awake; I am like a lonely bird on the housetop.

Is 37:25. I dried up with the sole of my foot all the streams of Egypt.

Mt 26:53. Do you think that I cannot appeal to my Father, and he will at once send me more than twelve legions of angels?

1Cor 15:10. But by the grace of God I am what I am, and his grace toward me has not been in vain. On the contrary, I worked harder than any of them—though it was not I, but the grace of God, that is with me.

Phil 2:13. For it is God who is at work in you, enabling you both to will and to work for his good pleasure.

Jn 15:5. I am the vine, you are the branches. Those who abide in me and I in them bear much fruit, because apart from me you can do nothing.

Ps 127:1–2. Unless the LORD builds the house, those who build it labor in vain. Unless the LORD guards the city, the guard keeps watch in vain. It is in vain that you rise up early and go late to rest, eating the bread of anxious toil; for he gives to sleep to his beloved.

Rom 9: 16. So it depends not on human will or exertion, but on God who shows mercy.

Jas 1:17. Every generous act of giving, with every perfect gift, is from above, coming down from the Father of lights, with whom there is no variation or shadow due to change.

1Cor 4:7. For who sees anything different in you? What do you have that you did not receive? And if you received it, why do you boast as if it were not a gift?

Ps 89:19. Then you spoke in a vision to your faithful one and said: "I have set the crown on one who is mighty, I have exalted one chosen from the people."

Mt 7:7. Ask, and it will be given you; search, and you will find; knock, and the door will be opened for you.

Ps 90:17. Let the favor of the Lord our God be upon us, and prosper for us the work of our hands—O prosper the work of our hands!

Ps 68:28. Summon your might O God; show your strength, O God, as you have done for us before.

Jn 5:30 and 14:10. I can do nothing on my own (5:30). The Father who dwells in me does his works (14:0).

Ps 118:13–14. I was pushed hard, so that I was falling, but the LORD helped me. The LORD is my strength and my might; he has become my salvation.

Ps 94: 17–19. If the LORD had not been my help, my soul would soon have lived in the land of silence. When I thought, "My foot is slipping," your steadfast love, O LORD, held me up. When the cares of my heart are many, your consolations cheer my soul.

Ps 18:1–3. ¹I love you, O LORD, my strength. ²The LORD is my rock, my fortress, and my deliverer, my God, my rock in whom I take refuge, my shield, and the horn of my salvation, my stronghold. ³I call upon the LORD, who is worthy to be praised, so I shall be saved from my enemies.

Ps 44:5–7. ⁵Through you we push down our foes; through your name we tread down our assailants. ⁶For not in my bow do I trust, nor can my sword save me. ⁷But you have put to confusion those who hate us.

Ps 35: 2–3. ²Take hold of shield and buckler, and rise up to help me! ³Draw the spear and javelin against my pursuers; say to my soul, "I am your salvation."

Ps 44:3. For not by their own sword did they win the land, nor did their own arm give them victory; but your right hand and your arm, and the light of your countenance, for you delighted in them.

Phil 2:6–8. ⁶Who, though he was in the form of God, did not regard equality with God as something to be exploited, ⁷but emptied himself, taking the form of a slave, being born in human likeness. And being found in human form, ⁸he humbled himself and became obedient to the point of death—even death on a cross.

Is 66:2. All these things my hand has made, and so all these things are mine, says the LORD. But his is the one to whom I will look, to the humble and contrite in spirit, who trembles at my word.

Humility

Prv 11:2. When pride comes, then comes disgrace; but wisdom is with the humble.

Prv 29:23. A person's pride will bring humiliation, but one who is lowly in spirit will obtain honor.

Ps 34:2. My soul makes its boast in the LORD; let the humble hear and be glad.

Phil 2:3. Do nothing from selfish ambition or conceit, but in humility regard others as better than yourselves.

Col 3:12. As God's chosen ones, holy and beloved, clothe yourselves with compassion, kindness, humility, meekness, and patience.

1Cor 1:27–31. ²⁷But God chose what is foolish in the world to shame the wise; God chose what is weak in the world to shame the strong; ²⁸God chose what is low and despised in the world, things that are not, to reduce to nothing things that are, ²⁹so that no one might boast in the presence of God. ³⁰He is the source of your life in Christ Jesus, who became for us wisdom from God, and righteousness and sanctification and redemption, ³¹in order that, as it is written, "Let the one who boasts, boast in the Lord."

Gal 6:14. May I never boast of anything except the cross of our Lord Jesus Christ, by which the world has been crucified to me, and I to the world.

Jn 3:30. He must increase, but I must decrease.

Authority (elders), humility, watchfulness

1Pt 5:5–11. ⁵In the same way, you who are younger must accept the authority of the elders. And all of you must clothe yourselves with humility in your dealings with one another, for "God opposes the proud, but gives grace to the humble." ⁶Humble yourselves therefore under the mighty hand of God, so that he may exalt you in due time. ⁷Cast all your anxiety on him, because he cares for you. ⁸Discipline yourselves, keep alert. Like a roaring lion your adversary the devil prowls around, looking for someone to devour. ⁹Resist him steadfast in your faith, for you know that your brothers and sisters in all the world are undergoing the same kinds of suffering. ¹⁰And after you have suffered for a little while, the God of all grace, who has called you to his eternal glory in Christ, will himself restore support, strengthen, and establish you. ¹¹To him be the power forever and ever. Amen.

The quotation in vs. 6 is from Prv 3:34.

Acceptance of suffering/affliction

Dt 8:2–3. ²Remember the long way that the LORD your God has led you these forty years in the wilderness, in order to humble you, testing you to know what was in your heart, whether or not you would keep his commandments. ³He humbled you by letting you hunger, then by feeding you with manna, with which neither you nor your ancestors were acquainted in order to make you understand that one does not live by bread alone, but by every word that comes from the mouth of the LORD.

Heb 12:7. Endure trials for the sake of discipline. God is treating you as children; for what child is there whom a parent does not discipline?

Rev 3:19. I reprove and discipline those whom I love. Be earnest therefore, and repent.

All is gift

Jn 3:27. John answered, "No one can receive anything except what has been given from heaven."

1Cor 4:7. For who sees anything different in you? What do you have that you did not receive? And if you received it, why do you boast as if it were not a gift?

Eph 2:8–10. ⁸For by grace you have been saved through faith, and this is not your own doing; it is the gift of God—⁹not the result of works, so that no one may boast. ¹⁰For we are what he has made us, created in Christ Jesus for good works, which God prepared beforehand to be our way of life.

1Cor 3:7. Neither the one who plants nor the one who waters is anything, but only God who gives the growth.

Mt 10:8. Cure the sick, raise the dead, cleanse the lepers, cast out demons. You received without payment; give without payment.

Preeminence of Christ

Jn 3:31. The one who comes from above is above all; the one who is of the earth belongs to the earth and speaks about earthly things. The one who comes from heaven is above all.

Jn 1:18. No one has ever seen God. It is God the only Son, who is close to the Father's heart who has made him known.

Col 1:19. For in him all the fullness of God was pleased to dwell.

Heb 1:3. He is the reflection of God's glory and the exact imprint of God's very being, and he sustains all things by his powerful word. When he had made purification for sins, he sat down at the right hand of the Majesty on high.

Phil 2:9–11. [9]Therefore God also highly exalted him and gave him the name that is above every name, [10] so that at the name of Jesus every knee should bend, in heaven and on earth and under the earth [11]and every tongue should confess that Jesus Christ is Lord, to the glory of God the Father.

Mk 15:37–39. [37]Then Jesus gave a loud cry and breathed his last. [38]And the curtain of the temple was torn in two, from top to bottom. [39]Now when the centurion, who stood facing him, saw that in this way he breathed his last, he said, "Truly this man was God's Son!"

Acknowledgments

Deo Gratias, I hope you can see the fruit of your collaboration:

Carol Falkner, O.S.B., and my Benedictine community at Beech Grove; Mary Sue Freiberger, O.S.B.; Kathleen Deignan, CND; Msgr. Michael L. Fitzgerald, M.Afr.; Jeanne Knoerle, S.P.; Colleen Mathews; Toddy and Dan Daly; Monika Clare Ghosh; Jim and Marina Funk; Shahid Athar, MD; Thomas Funk, O.D.; Abbot Laurence O'Keefe, O.S.B.; Odette Leger, SC; William Skudlarek, O.S.B.; Bridget Funk; Nicholas Benner; Tom Widner, S.J.; John Borelli, PhD.; James Wiseman, O.S.B.; Columba Stewart, O.S.B.; Judith Cebula; Julie Thompson; Louisville Institute; Magdalena FitzGibbon, O.S.B.; Our Lady of the Mississippi Trappistines; Don and Aline Funk; Frank Oveis and the Continuum International Publishing Group; and His Holiness the Dalai Lama.

Notes

1. For more reading about the desert tradition I recommend taking the chronological sources. Start with the gospels, then the sayings, lives, conferences and finally the rules.

For the Gospels:

The Holy Bible, New Revised Standard Version containing the Old and New Testaments with the Apocryphal/Deuterocanonical Books.

For the Sayings:

The Sayings of the Desert Fathers: The Alphabetical Collection. Trans. Benedicta Ward, S.L.G. Cistercian Studies Series, no. 59. Kalamazoo, MI: Cistercian Publications, 1975. This is a Greek collection in which the sayings of each father are grouped under his name and arranged alphabetically.

The Wisdom of the Desert. Comp. Thomas Merton. New York: New Directions, 1960. A collection of Merton's favorite sayings from the *Verbum Senorium* (Latin) collection of desert father sayings.

The Wisdom of the Desert Fathers: Apophthegmata Patrum from the Anonymous Series. Trans. Benedicta Ward, S.L.G. Kalamazoo, MI: Cistercian Publications, 1975. A translation of the Greek collection *Apophthegmata Patrum: Anonymous Series;* the sayings are arranged by subject.

For the Lives:

Palladius. *The Lausiac History.* Trans. Robert T. Meyer. Ancient Christian Writers Series, no. 4. New York: Paulist Press, 1965. A fifth-century description of desert fathers and mothers in Egypt, Palestine, Syria, and Asia Minor.

For Anthony:

Athanasius. *The Life of Anthony and the Letter to Marcellinus.* Trans. Robert C. Gregg. Classics of Western Spirituality. New York: Paulist Press, 1980. This influential fourth-century work could be considered the first handbook in the Christian ascetical tradition.

For Basil:
The Fathers Speak: St. Basil the Great, St. Gregory of Naziazen, St. Gregory of Nyssa: Selected Letters and Life-Records. Trans. Georges A. Barrois. Crestwood, NY: St. Valdimir's Seminary Press, 1986.

For John Cassian:
Thomas Merton. *Cassian and the Fathers: Initiation into the Monastic Tradition.* Ed. Patrick F. O'Connell.Kalamazoo, MI: Cistercian Publications, 2005.

Columba Stewart. *Cassian the Monk.* New York: Oxford University Press, 1998. A thorough discussion of Cassian's teaching on the theory and practice of monastic asceticism.

For Pachomius:
The Lives, Rules, and Other Writings of St. Pachomius and His Disciples. 1: The Life of St. Pachomius and His Disciples; II: Rule; III: Other Writings. Trans. Armand Veilleux. Cistercian Studies 45–47. Kalamazoo, MI: Cistercian Publications, 1980–1982. The story of Pachomius, founder of monastic communal (conobitic) life characterized by shared labor and liturgy.

For Conferences by the Desert Fathers:
John Cassian. *Conferences.* Trans. Boniface Ramsey, O.P. Ancient Christian Writers, no. 57. New York: Newman/Paulist Press, l997. Cassian's dialogues with the great desert masters on the practice of the spiritual life.

John Climacus. *The Ladder of Divine Ascent.* Trans. Colm Luibheid and Norman Russell. Classics of Western Spirituality. New York: Paulist Press, 1982.

For the Eight Thoughts:
John Cassian. *The Institutes.* Trans. Boniface Ramsey, O.P. Ancient Christian Writers, no 58. New York: Newman/Paulist Press, 2000. Cassian's record of the rules of monastic life in Egypt and lessons on struggles against the eight thoughts.

For the Rule of St. Benedict:
Terrence G. Kardong, O.S.B. *Benedict's Rule: A Translation and Commentary.* Collegeville, MN: Liturgical Press, 1996. Literal translation from the Latin, but faithful to Benedict's use of words. The commentary, while scholarly, is practical to living the monastic life.

Aquinata Bockmann, O.S.B. *Perspectives on the Rule of Saint Benedict.* Collegeville, MN: Liturgical Press, 2005. A critical edition for scholars, but readable and inspiring commentary on Benedict's School of the Lord's Service, good zeal, seeking God, stability, and hospitality.

2. *Lectio divina* is a prayer form using sacred texts. It interweaves scripture, nature, and our life events. Scripture informs experience, which in turn opens wide the senses to receive nature. The reader encounters the text at levels from the literal to the mystical depths. The reader is primarily a listener and the text is a teacher that has a tradition to transmit to the disciple.

There is no single method for the prayer form of *lectio divina*. It is the culture of a contemplative. As a prayer form it must be learned and practiced. Week-long sessions to learn *lectio divina* and to live the contemplative life with Our Lady of Grace Monastery are available through the School of *Lectio Divina*, Benedict Inn, Beech Grove, IN 46107. www.benedictine. com

3. Tradition holds that there is also baptism of desire, wherein one intends to follow Christ but has no opportunity for baptism.

4. *Breaking Bread* (Portland: Oregon Catholic Press, 2005), p. 80.

5. Ibid., p. 84

6. John Cassian, *Conferences*, trans. Boniface Ramsey, Ancient Christian Writers, no. 57 (New York: Newman/Paulist Press, 1997), 9.5.6, p. 324.

7. Mary Margaret Funk, *Tools Matter for Practicing the Spiritual Life* (New York: Continuum, 2003), p. 52.

8. I'm aware that in some traditions the words *continence* and *chastity* are interchangeable and also used for all aspects of the virtuous life and not just sexual purity. But it's helpful for our generation to see the progression of how thoughts move from outer circumstances to inner dispositions.

9. Celibacy traditionally is the term for no-sex as in a state of life for a monk or a nun. I am using it to refer to the middle term between continence and chastity. While continence is no-sex and chastity is no thought in the heart about sex, there is a need for a middle term to explain how married persons are chaste according to their commitment. I'm using the word *celibacy* for commitment according to one's vocation, or calling. The most comprehensive book on chastity in Cassian's writing is Columba Stewart's book, *Cassian the Monk*. While he uses the traditional terms for continence, celibacy, and chastity, it was in reading Father Columba's fine book that I grasped the distinctions and also understood that chastity is not a vocation that is given to each of us, but a practice that each of us has to cultivate to live a chaste life.

10. I'm aware that in other faith traditions there are lay monastics who are also married and ordained monastics who are householders. The teaching is the same: celibacy except with married partner.

11. Thomas Merton, *Cassian and the Fathers: Invitation into the Monastic Tradition*, ed. Patrick F. O'Connell, Monastic Wisdom Series, no. 1 (Kalamazoo, MI: Cistercian Publications, 2005), pp. 179–80.

12. Thomas Merton, "The Cell," in *Contemplation in a World of Action* (Garden City, NY: Doubleday, 1971), pp. 252–59.

13. Benedicta Ward, *Harlots of the Desert: A Study of Repentance in Early Monastic Sources* (Kalamazoo, MI: Cistercian Publications, 1987), p. 11. This study takes five women and shows how repentance purifies and sanctifies all manner of former way of life. To sort out just who was Mary Magdalene I found this paragraph helpful: "The name, Mary of Magdala, is found in Luke 8.2 and Mark 16.9. In Luke she is one of the women who followed Jesus, 'out of whom he had cast seven devils', and in Mark again she is 'a woman out of whom he had cast seven devils', but she is also the one to whom he first appeared after his resurrection. This gives us a Mary from Magdala, a woman possessed by seven devils (in other words, a woman who was cured of the sickness of sin by Jesus): a forgiven sinner who followed him in his ministry and met him after he rose from the dead. In the gospel of John, Mary Magdalene is named in two situations, first with the mother of Jesus at the foot of the cross, and second in a more extended account of her meeting with Jesus in the garden of the resurrection (John 19.25; 20.1–19). So far the picture is consistent enough: Mary Magdalene cured; a disciple; someone present at the crucifixion; a witness of the resurrection and according to John, the first to take the news of the Lord's resurrection to the apostles. Luke also says that she was among the women who anointed the Lord's body for burial (Luke 24.10). Mary Magdalene is a model of ceaseless repentance."

14. Merton, *Cassian*, pp. 182–83.

15. Ibid., p. 193.

16. *The Cloud of Unknowing and the Book of Privy Counseling*, ed. William Johnston (New York: Image Books, 1973), p. 48.

17. Funk, *Tools Matter,* p. 116.

18. I asked an Orthodox nun why some of the better passages of John Cassian were not in the *Philokalia.* She said that the compilation of texts for the *Philokalia* are intended for beginners and that when the *staretz* says the disciple is ready then they can read the more esoteric texts. There is a profound respect when "the Other" has been part of the inner experience that fits this third renunciation: to renounce one's self-made thoughts about God and also to renounce one's thoughts about one's experience of God. God is God and my experience of God is my experience. I know and am known.

19. *The Cloud of Unknowing and the Book of Privy Counseling*, p. 152.

20. "Selfing to sacrifice." This is an invented phrase to express the dynamism of the shift. To be self-centered seems deterministic, so I've used the term *selfing,* the gerund that expresses the ongoing nature of reversing self-

centeredness. I suppose it is the same distinction of *conversatio* and *conversio*. *Conversatio* denotes the ongoing nature of conversion and the word *conversio* is usually the sudden event of conversion that initiates the shift from one's former way of life. Benedictines take a vow of *conversatio morum* as a way of life.

21. Funk, *Tools Matter*, p. 102.

22. Thérèse of Lisieux, *Story of a Soul: The Autobiography of St. Thérèse of Lisieux*, trans. John Clarke (Washington: ICS Publications, 1996), pp. 97–99.

23. Ibid., p. 168.

24. Ibid., pp. 276–77.

25. Ibid., p. 207ff.

26. Patrick Ahern, *Maurice and Thérèse: The Story of a Love* (New York: Doubleday, 1998), p. 114.

27. John Cassian, *Institutes*, p. 3.

28. Ibid., p. 100

29. Merton, *Cassian and the Fathers*, p. 155. Merton's summary of Cassian's ten degrees of humility:

a) The mortification of all our desires;
b) The manifestation of all our acts and thoughts to the Spiritual Father;
c) To do nothing by our own judgment but in all to submit our judgment to the Spiritual Father;
d) In all things to be obedient and meek and constant in patience;
e) Do no injury to anyone and to accept injuries without sadness;
f) To do nothing that is not indicated by the common rule or the examples of the seniors;
g) To be content with everything that is lowest and to do what one is commanded considering himself an unworthy and useless servant;
h) Not only to call oneself the worst of all but to believe in one's inmost heart that it is so;
i) To restrain one's tongue and not to be a loud-speaker;
j) To be *facilis et promptus in risu* (to be quick to laugh).

30. Cassian, *Institutes*, p. 99.

31. Cassian, *Conferences*, p. 337.

32. Ibid.

33. Funk, *Tools Matter*, p. 52.

34. Cassian, *Institutes*, p. 102.

35. Ann Deignan, "Grace," from her poetry collection, *Migration* (Mt. Carmel, CT: Schola Ministries, 2003), p. 5. Used with permission.

36. Psychic imprint is a way of saying that each of us has a deeply felt and essential form that recognizes what "fits" regarding a manifestation of

God or spirituality. For me as a Christian, it is the God-shaped hole that finds the Christ Jesus of my baptism. This psychic imprint is my particularity. When I come home to my deepest self I know it.

37. I am aware that the technical term *kenosis* is reserved for the awesome fact that Christ, who was divine, emptied himself of his divinity for our sakes. This meditation simply refers to the fact that we can imitate Christ's kenosis through the low doors of humility, emptying ourselves and embracing the whole of the human condition. What Christ did (kenosis) of his divinity, we do through the four renunciations.

38. I asked Colleen Mathews to research this scripture account of Jesus being angry, since whenever I teach the affliction of anger this always comes as a challenging counterpoint to Cassian's "be not angry" dictum. I edited this study from a much larger text to give readers a sense of the richness and complexity of the scriptural texts that report this significant event.

39. Colleen Mathews did the primary research on this compilation of references on the eight afflictions in the Hebrew and Christian scriptures. We had prepared this document for a workbook that was to accompany *Tools Matter.* I have used these scripture quotes to help persons do *lectio divina* in the areas where they are suffering from one of the afflictions. I am grateful for Colleen Mathews' permission to offer her study for the benefit of readers of *Humility Matters.*

Select Bibliography

Abhishiktananda. *Prayer*. I.S.P.C.K. 1993.

The Art of Prayer: An Orthodox Anthology. Comp. Igumen Chariton of Valamo. Trans. E. Kadloubovsky and E. M. Palmer. Ed. Timothy Ware. London: Faber and Faber, 1966.

Benedict of Nursia. *RB 1980: The Rule of St. Benedict in Latin and English with Notes*. Ed. Timothy Fry, O.S.B. Collegeville, MN: Liturgical Press, 1996. A modern English translation of Benedict's sixth-century Rule with the Latin text, explanatory notes, topical essays, indexes, and a Latin concordance. A small English-only edition without the scholarly additions is also available. The degrees of humility found in chapter 7 are a classic description of spiritual growth in Christ.

Bernard of Clairvaux. *Bernard of Clairvaux, A Lover Teaching the Way of Love: Selected Spiritual Writings*. Ed. M. Basil Pennington. New York: New City Press, 1997. This collection includes St. Bernard's commentary on St. Benedict's twelve degrees of humility.

Cassian, John. *Conferences*. Trans. Bonifice Ramsey, O.P. Ancient Christian Writers, no. 57. New York: Newman/Paulist Press, 1997. Cassian's dialogues with the great desert masters on the practice on the spiritual life.

Cassian, John. *The Institutes*. Trans. Boniface Ramsey, O.P. Ancient Christian Writers, no. 58. New York: Newman/Paulist Press, 2000. Cassian's record of the rules of monastic life in Egypt and lessons on struggles against the eight thoughts.

Chryssavgis, John. *In the Heart of the Desert: The Spirituality of the Desert Fathers and Mothers*. Bloomington, IN: World Wisdom, 2003. A thorough and thoughtful introduction to the lives and teachings of the desert fathers and mothers.

Clément, Oliver. *The Roots of Christian Mysticism*. New York: New City Press, 1995. Carefully chosen texts and reflections revealing the early church's experience, including humility and faith related to the personal presence of the mystery of Christ.

Climacus, John. *The Ladder of Divine Ascent*. Trans. Colm Luibheid and Norman Russell. Classics of Western Spirituality. New York: Paulist

Press, 1982. This instruction on the ascetic practice portrays the spiritual life as a ladder that the aspirant must ascend. Its thirty steps represent the hidden, humble life of Christ.

Dreuille, Mayeul de, O.S.B. *The Rule of Benedict and the Ascetic Traditions from Asia to the West*. Trans. Mayeul de Dreuille, O.S.B., and Mark Hargreaves, O.S.B., England: MPG Books, 2000 (new edition distributed by Liturgical Press). This book takes humility as one of the monastic themes that is the path of mystics in Hindu, Buddhist, Sufi, and Christian traditions.

Matthew the Poor. *The Communion of Love*. Crestwood, NY: St. Vladimir's Seminary Press, 1984. This collection of writings includes the themes of humility, repentance, asceticism, and fasting.

Merton, Thomas. *Cassian and the Fathers: Initiation into the Monastic Tradition*. Ed. Patrick F. O'Connell. Monastic Wisdom Series, no. 1. Kalamazoo, MI: Cistercian Publications, 2005. This is Thomas Merton's lectures to the monks at Gethsemani. Has excellent notes and context written by Patrick Hart, Colomba Stewart, and Patrick O'Connell.

Philokalia: The Complete Text, vols. 1–4. Comp. St. Nikidemos of the Holy Mountain and St. Makarios of Corinth. Trans. and ed. G. E. H. Palmer, Philip Sherrad, and Kallistos Ware. London: Faber and Faber, 1979–1995. An anthology of the spiritual writings of the early fathers. This is the primary source for all the teachings on the Jesus Prayer.

The Syriac Fathers on Prayer and the Spiritual Life. Trans. Sebastian Brock. Kalamazoo, MI: Cistercian Publications, 1987.

Vlachos, Hierotheos S. *Orthodox Psychotherapy: The Science of the Fathers*. Trans. Esther Williams. Levadia, Greece: Birth of Theotokos Monastery, 1994. A presentation of the teachings of the fathers on the cure of the soul from the problems of thoughts and a darkened mind.

Ware, Kallistos. *The Inner Kingdom: Collected Works*. Vol. 1. Crestwood, NY: St. Vladimir's Seminary Press, 2000. The first of a series of the collected works from a well-known Eastern Orthodox bishop. Of particular interest in relation to the theme of humility are essays on repentance and the ascetic tradition of Orthodoxy.